Also, by Joseph Michael Sepesy

Word Dances: A Collection of Verses and Thoughts about Ballroom Dancing

Word Dances II: Your Time to Dance

Word Dances III: Celebration

Word Dances IV: The Romance of the Dance

Word Dances V: The World of Social Ballroom Dancing through Short Stories, Thoughts, and Verse

The Relic of Domremy

The Flight of St. Joan's Cross, The Relic of Domremy, Part II

Once We Flew

Volume II: Aftermath

The Memoir of a US Army Helicopter Pilot in Vietnam and a Life with PTSD

Joseph Michael Sepesy

ISBN: 978-1-7948-1059-4 (sc)
ISBN: 978-1-7948-1056-3 (e)

Library of Congress Control Number: 2021920553

Lulu Publishing Services rev. date: 11/12/2021

Cover Images

Helicopter at sunset, author's private collection.

US Army Aviator Wings (Courtesy of the US Army).

Once We Flew, a Dedication

To the veterans of the Vietnam War who wore the silver wings
of US Army Aviation.

Once we flew, facing unknown challenges and dangers ... and yes, our own uncertainties and fears of war and combat.

Drawing upon youthful energy and inexperience, with desire and a daring demeanor—we stepped forward.

Our innate abilities were enhanced and perfected, honed and polished—we struggled, learned and progressed.

Guided by history and example, tradition and allegiance, we prevailed and succeeded, we celebrated—wings earned.

Armed with confidence and courage, tempered by training and common sense—we adjusted, grew stronger, and soared.

We witnessed reality, character and truth, discovered trust and loyalty, with every mission flown and completed.

Inspired by a sense of duty, we performed for country and unit, and for fellow warriors flying with us—we sacrificed.

We experienced accomplishment and satisfaction, pride and victory—recalling loss and sorrow—touching wounds and scars.

We survived, dedicated patriots, forever bound by that powerful and inexplicable love, best expressed as "a band of brothers."

Yes … *once we flew.*

(Photo credit, previous page: US Army aviator wings, pilot and crewmember, courtesy of the US Army.)

Contents

(Note: Parts 1 through 6 appear in *Once We Flew, Volume 1.*)

Part 7

Veteran

17 February 1973: Happy Birthday, Mom!... 1

February 1973: Killing the Enemy and Taking Fire 4

February 1973: Awards and Decorations, and Patches 6

February 1973: Re-acclimation 9

29 July 1973 to 2 June 1974: Weekend Warrior 12

Winter 1974: Poetry... 16

Early 1975: Prophecy Fulfilled 19

The Cost—US Army Aviation 21

September 1973 to August 1977: Student, Youngstown State
University—PTSD, Part 1 23

21 January 1977: A Slap in the Face.. 27

23 August 1977 to 16 August 1978: Flying in the Gulf of Mexico—
PTSD, Part 2 29

Summer 1978: The Flyer-Philosopher.. 39

September 1978: Teaching—PTSD, Part 3 41

October 1978: Ducking for Cover—PTSD, Part 4.. 49

Winter 1981: Return to Active Duty … but only Briefly 52

Winter 1982: Post-Traumatic Stress Disorder, Part 5 56

Spring 1983: A Local Parade 60

1984 and 1986 64

Summer, 1985: The Wall—PTSD, Part 6 66

25 December 1985: Honorable Discharge 68

1988: Demon Dreams—PTSD, Part 7 70

Memorial Day, 1991: The Salute 72

Summer 1991: Living Vicariously 74

February 1992: The Rest of the Story 75

7 September 1993: Mom Died Today—PTSD, Part 8 77

1994: Cronkite Was Wrong, Schwarzkopf Was Right! 79

Autumn 1994: An Incredible Chance Meeting 82

1998: My Demon Dreams Continue—PTSD, Part 9 85

March 2000 and 22 August 2000: Masher Huey 048 87

Veterans Day, 2001: On the Air 93

26 December 2001: The Greatest Generation Gathers at the Kitchen Table 96

Summer 2002: Jackie and I Visit Motts Military Museum 98

Veterans Day, 2002: On the Air Again at Y-103 100

9 January 2003: Bobby Cowen Died Today 102

17 March 2003: Operation Iraqi Freedom 104

31 March 2003: An Announcement 106

2 May 2003: Induction, Ohio Military Hall of Fame for Valor 108

Summer 2003: Aftermath 112

Veterans Day, 2003: Third Time on the Airwaves at Y-103 114

February and March 2004: Back Operations 3 and 4 115

June 2004: I Cried—PTSD, Part 10 117

August 2004: The Best Reunion—Band of Brothers, Part 4 120

Veterans Day, 2004: Y-103, the Fourth Time 124

December 2004: Stolen Valor.. 128

June 2005: Four Masher Aircraft Commanders—Band of Brothers, Part 5 ... 130

9 November 2005: Fifth Appearance on Y-103 134

Part 8

Transformations

February 2006: Getting Help—PTSD, Part 11 143

2 April 2006: Mike Novosel Died Today 145

July 2006: VHPA Reunion, Washington DC—Band of Brothers, Part 6 146

November 2006: Group Counseling—PTSD, Part 12 151

6 July 2007: At Motts Military Museum with Randy Clark—Band of
Brothers, Part 7 154

July 2008: More Demon Dreams—PTSD, Part 13 159

July 2008: *The* Epiphany 162

Summer 2008: Confessions—PTSD, Part 14.................................... 165

September 1978 to February 2009—My Thirty-One-Year War Comes
to an End—PTSD, Part 15.. 168

2009: Private Matters—PTSD, Part 16 177

7 and 8 March 2009: Louisville, Kentucky....................................178

11 June 2009: Crazy Horse, Masher Huey 545 181

15 June 2009: Uncle Frank Died Today—PTSD, Part 17 183

2009: It Still Hurts—PTSD, Part 18... 186

1 to 4 July 2009: VHPA Reunion, Philadelphia—Band of Brothers, Part 8 ... 188

15 July and 30 September 2009: Reunited with Mr. Clean—Band of
Brothers, Part 9 191

November 2009: Talk the Talk, Walk the Walk ... Dance the Dance—
PTSD, Part 19 197

Autumn 2000 through Spring 2010: Parking Lot Man, PTSD, Part 20.......... 202

13 through 16 May 2010: With Mr. Clean at the Wall—Band of
Brothers, Part 10 206

September 2010: Dear Mom—PTSD Part 21... 209

24 January 2012: Dad Died Today..213

1 July 2013: At Arlington National Cemetery—Band of Brothers, Part 11......218

13 March 2015: Jackie Earns Her Wings.. 221

30 October 2016: Mr. Clean Died Today—Band of Brothers, Part 12............. 222

Youth—Band of Brothers, Part 13 224

Perspective will come in retrospect.

—Melody Beattie, inspiringquotes.us

Epilogue

Final Thoughts: Flight, PTSD, Life ... and Dance

A Transformed Life 231

Veterans Day, 2017: You Could Hear a Pin Drop—PTSD, Part 22 235

Mistakes and Regrets... 243

Spring, 2018: Final Puzzle Pieces.. 247

2019: Living with PTSD, Part 23... 250

19 October 2019: Linda and I Are Married.. 253

1970 ad Infinitum: Some Things Will Always Be the Same—PTSD, Part 24..... 260

Memories, a Verse 264

A Final Eulogy.. 266

Present Day: Coming Full Circle and Final *Ponderments* 269

Present Day: Coming Full Circle and Final *Ponderments*, Part 2 270

Final Transmission.. 273

Addendum

Acknowledgments 275

Chronology of Military Service 279

Valorous Unit Award 282

Letter of Appreciation from Headquarters, 7th Squadron, 17th Cavalry........... 283

Recommended Reading List... 284

PTSD was not officially recognized by the *Diagnostic and Statistical Manual of Mental Disorders,* a publication of the American Psychiatric Association, in 1980, after years of research beginning in early 1977.

Introduction—Post-Traumatic Stress Disorder (PTSD)

The main subtheme of this book is PTSD (Post-Traumatic Stress Disorder), something I am very familiar with, having endured this condition from the time I left Vietnam to the present. The reader will find epigraphs—some as lead-ins that preface entries, and some as reinforcements at the end of entries.

I hope to educate the reader, in a lay fashion, about PTSD—which may prove helpful for him or her, or for someone in the reader's life, suspected of having PTSD. Such knowledge could improve the sufferer's quality of life, and those closest to him or her, and could even save a life. The following epigraphs reinforce this notion.

> *My work on The Trion Syndrome has persuaded me that the time is long past for us to change the terminology we use to designate combat stress—which I personally suffer from. The term "Post-Traumatic Stress Disorder" (PTSD) suggests that the condition is an internal malfunction, something gone awry in the brain or mind. "Disorder" can carry the connotation that the victim is subject to the disease through weakness or inborn deficiency or even cowardice. Yet those who have experienced combat are among the strongest and bravest people on earth. Their reaction is healthy...*
> *"Post-Traumatic Stress Injury" (PTSI) expresses the undeniable fact that an external force has inflicted damage. The latter is far more precise and reflects reality....*
> *I've been using "PTSI" for some years now, and I think it's time to push for the use of that term. I'll be doing so every chance I get.*
>
> —Tom Glenn, Facebook, 17 July 2015

You have to understand that PTSD has to be an event that you experience, a very traumatic event. And actually, there is evidence that brain chemistry changes during this event in certain individuals where it's imprinted indelibly forever and there's an emotion associated with this which triggers the condition.

—Dale Archer, picturequotes.com

I'm not a doctor, nor am I a member of the military. What I am is an appreciative, concerned American citizen, who was horrified when I heard about the horrendous rates of suicide (22 per day) and PTSD/TBI within our military. As such, I felt compelled to reach out to anyone who cared to listen, to try to help with this terrible situation. This is not just life and death - it is life and death for those who defend our freedom.

—Ken Wahl, idlehearts.com

Bad things do happen; how I respond to them defines my character and the quality of life. I can choose to sit in perpetual sadness, immobilized by the gravity of my loss, or I can choose to rise from the pain and treasure the most precious gift I have—life itself.

—Walter Anderson, brainyquote.com

In 2010, an estimated sixty percent of Vietnamese people and thirty-five percent of Americans living today were born after the Vietnam War ended in April 1975.

"My yesterdays walk with me. They keep step, they are gray faces that peer over my shoulder."

—William Golding, brainyquote.com

Author's Notes

Assistance

For the reader's convenience, I have provided lists of information before the body of the text that will assist reading and understanding. That information includes lists of Acronyms, Abbreviations and Terms, Pronunciation Key, and Numerical Designations; followed by maps of Indochina, Military Regions III Corps, and II Corps.

Epigraphs

For enhancement, one or more epigraphs appear at the top of each chronological entry. All provide information or offer insight relevant to this memoir. They include images, quotations, song lyrics, and historical notations.

Epigraphs on the left speak to aviation, the author's personal military service, images and quotations—all pertinent to the entry they precede. Epigraphs on the right provide historical or factual notations about Vietnam and US military history, as well as other images and quotations.

Some epigraphs appear after an entry, separated from the text with sequences of asterisks: ** PTSD ** or ** Dance **. These epigraphs speak only to PTSD (Post-Traumatic Stress Disorder), reinforcing the content of the preceding entry and foreshadowing the consequences that PTSD had on me, or to the transformative effect ballroom dancing has had on my life.

Some epigraphs offer humor or present food for thought. Some present contradictions or opposing points of view. A handful may be unpleasant, offering dark humor.

Criticisms

The reader will see that I am critical of the tactics used by some US Army aviation companies I encountered during my second and third tours of duty in Vietnam. I do not intend to besmirch the individual skills and courage of the vast majority of their pilots. However, their procedures and practices employed during flight were without question, unnecessarily dangerous and potentially deadly in consequence—therefore worthy of criticism.

Some units regularly flew in the kill zone, and their flights lacked integrity during combat assault missions. Such propensities needlessly jeopardized the safety of crews and passengers. Such practices are the sources of my initial admonishments.

I am also critical of individuals, whose names I have changed. I have characterized those individuals accurately. To present less would diminish the impact of the occurrences described in this memoir.

Whatever protestations may be leveled, whatever consternation arises or outrage is voiced, understand—I know what I encountered and witnessed and relate those experiences without exaggeration.

Humor

Throughout this book the reader will find and one-word inscription, Josy , placed in either obvious or obscure parts of a page and on images. I provide its explanation in Part 2 of *Volume I's* text. Enjoy.

Freedom Is Not Free

I watched the flag pass by one day—it fluttered in the breeze. A young man in uniform saluted it, and then he stood at ease.

I looked at him in uniform—so young, so tall, so proud, with hair cut square and eyes alert, he'd stand out in the crowd.

I thought how many men like him had fallen through the years? How many died on foreign soil? How many mother's tears? How many pilots' planes shot down? How many foxholes were soldiers' graves?

No, freedom is not free.

I heard the sound of "Taps" one night, when everything was still, I listened to the bugler play and felt a sudden chill I wondered just how many times that "Taps" had meant, "Amen," when a flag had draped a coffin of a brother or a friend.

I thought of all the children, of mothers and the wives, of fathers, sons and husbands, with interrupted lives. I thought about a graveyard at the bottom of the sea, of unmarked graves in Arlington.

No, freedom is not free.

—Major Kelly Strong, yourdailypoem.com

Part 7

Veteran

A mother's love is instinctual, unconditional, and forever.

—Revathi Sankaran

17 February 1973: Happy Birthday, Mom!

No one knew I was coming home. The last anyone had heard anything from me was three weeks ago when I hurriedly wrote Mom and Dad a letter that contained little information. After processing out of the US Army in Oakland, California, I flew home to Youngstown, landing at the Vienna airport in brilliant sunshine and snow-covered ground.

The temperature was in the teens, and the wind was howling. Conversely, I was wearing my tropical-weight khakis and light flight jacket. My luggage missed the connector flight in Chicago, and I was told an airline employee would deliver it tomorrow. So, I grabbed my flight bag and walked out of the terminal.

I had trudged through the blowing snow only a few yards when a couple stopped their car and offered me a ride. I got in the back and after a few seconds we were on Route 193, heading south to Youngstown.

I told the driver that I was going to Catalina Avenue on the north side, right off of Belmont Avenue. "How far is that from Saint Elizabeth's Hospital?" he asked.

"Easy—about a mile past Catalina, on the right side."

This arrangement couldn't have been better, and twenty minutes later, I was thanking the couple for the lift as I left their car at the corner of Belmont and Catalina by the hardware store. I crossed Belmont and walked past the drugstore and the florist shop. I saw my brick house a short distance away, and my favorite tree. The wind continued to howl and bit at the exposed skin of my face, neck, and hands—I didn't care—I'd be home in three minutes.

It was about one o'clock in the afternoon when I quietly opened the back door and slipped inside. I wanted to surprise Mom and whoever else was home, but I didn't want to frighten anyone either.

I walked into the kitchen without saying a word. My beautiful sister, Kathy, was there baking a birthday cake for Mom. She saw me and froze in place. I hushed her with a finger to my lips; we stepped to each other, then we hugged—I was home.

"Where's Mom?"

"In her bedroom."

"Say something to get her into the kitchen."

Kathy nodded and called, "Mom, could you help me with this cake mix?"

"What's wrong?" answered Mom.

"I need help," said Kathy.

"Oh, all right, give me a second."

I was leaning against the sink as Mom entered the kitchen. I remember Mom was saying something to Kathy about the cake and putting her glasses on. She turned her head to her left and saw me standing there. I remember she stopped in her tracks and then it was her turn to freeze in place. She yelled! She yelled, "Joe!" disbelieving her eyes.

"Happy birthday, Mom," I said.

My words and Mom's own thought process confirmed what she was seeing. She quickly dismissed her disbelief and said, "Joe!" again and threw herself into my arms—I can still feel her tight embrace. We held each other close. Mom trembled and cried, and we just held each other for the longest time.

After the three of us calmed down, I explained how I was out of the Army and had made my way home. I think this was the best birthday present Mom could ever have received. That I was no longer in the Army relieved Mom and made her very happy—of that, I am sure.

When Dad came home from the three-to-eleven shift at Republic Steel, I was waiting in the living room, seated in a chair in the corner where the Christmas tree would stand every December. Dad walked in, but didn't notice me as quickly as Mom had. Actually, he did a double-take and in typical Dad fashion said, "What are you doing here?"

"I'm out of the Army," I said as I walked to Dad and gave him a hug.

This time there was no need for calming—Dad was just fine, surprised to see me, and disappointed that I had left the Army. He was hoping I would have made a career in the military.

I'm sure we talked about many things, but I distinctly remembering predicting that South Vietnam would fall in six months, after all US troops had gone.

Later that evening, after more discussion with my brothers and sisters. I realized a chapter of my life had ended and another was about to begin. It was very nice to be home again—but very different—the exact opposite of the summer of 1969, when I looked out my bedroom window onto the field where I once played war. Today my thoughts were about returning to civilian life. I wondered—*Did I do the right thing—getting out of the Army?*

On the lighter side, I realized that I would have to buy some new clothes and figure out where I would live. I also found out that Mom had thrown away all of my comic books—all of them; DC's *Green Lantern, Flash, the Justice League of America, Superman, Batman* … even my collection of *Classics Illustrated*!

***

With American out of Vietnam, NVA General Giap's plan was to invade the South. However, wanting to ensure complete victory and an optimum political position, he waited until March 1975 to begin his invasion. And, no one, including him, expected the entire South would fall by the end of April, after only six weeks.

12 February to 29 March 1973: 587 American POWs repatriated.

However, over 2,200 US servicemen remained unaccounted for.

29 March 1973: The last combat US troops left South Vietnam. Only a detachment of Marines remained, serving at the American embassy in Saigon.

24 October 1973: US intelligence reports indicated that since the cease-fire, the NVA increased its presence in the South by 70,000 troops, 400 tanks, and 200 artillery pieces. The NVA also constructed twelve airfields and an all-weather road from North Vietnam to Tay Ninh was nearing completion.

In 1973, with the end of the Vietnam War, the US Army deactivated Fort Wolters and consolidated all flight training at Fort Rucker, Alabama.

February 1973: Killing the Enemy and Taking Fire

Sometimes people ask me, in an uncertain or cautious manner, if I had ever killed enemy soldiers. Sometimes I would shoot a weapon out the window of a Huey using my .38 pistol, an M-16, or an old .45-caliber grease gun that floated around the company. I did so only when I could trust my Charlie Pop, and even then, that was taking a chance. If my Charlie Pop got shot, my reaction time for grabbing the controls would have been less effective.

So, did I kill any VC or NVA? Did I ever hit any enemy soldier? The answer is probably no. But I shot the hell out of a few trees—of that, I'm sure.

If fact, I only saw enemy soldiers running in the open twice, both during combat assaults. On one occasion I directed the gunner to their location as we were departing an LZ in Cambodia. Two guys in dark pajamas were hightailing it away from the commotion. The door gunner opened up on them, but he didn't hit them.

The other time was during my extension tour. While following that dim-witted Chickenman captain through the mountains in horrible weather. Not only did we take fire, but we saw a few little bastards hurrying to a tree line for cover while their buddies were shooting at us.

Flashes from tree lines or tracers arcing toward us and across our flight paths marked enemy fire. The time involved was a matter of seconds because retaliation from our cover birds was immediate and swift, which usually discouraged further enemy fire. And I'm sure I took fire more times than I can remember simply because it can't be heard much of the time and can't be seen, depending on where one's attention is occupied. There's too much noise in the cockpit from the engine and radios. Small-arms fire was a cracking or popping sound and fire from .51 cals was a low, throaty thumping.

** PTSD **

"Civilians understand soldiers to have a kind of baseline duty, and that everything above that is considered, 'bravery.' Soldiers see it the other way around; either you're doing your duty or you're a coward."

—Sebastian Junger, *War*, published by Twelve, 2010

27 January 1974: Since the signing of the truce one year ago; 13,788 South Vietnamese soldiers and 2,159 civilians; and 45,057 communist soldiers were killed.

"What is a Veteran?"

"A veteran, whether active duty, discharged, retired, or reserve is someone who, at one point in his life, wrote a blank check made payable to the United States of America, for an amount of, up to and including his life."

—"Thanking Our Veterans," US Department of Homeland Security, 7 November 2016

No purple heart for PTSD(I)I (Injury)? We need to change that! The invisible injury is still an injury.

—Brian Dell Beckstead, quozio.com

February 1973: Awards and Decorations, and Patches

There are three types of individual awards in the Army that I am familiar with: those for valor, those for achievement, and those for service.

During my four years in the Army, I received all three types of awards. Each award is a medal with its accompanying ribbon, a written order, and certificate. Medals are worn on dress uniforms and on the day that they are awarded. Ribbons are worn on the left side of the chest of dress uniforms and khakis. Some may bear oak leaf clusters, indicative of multiple awards of that medal. Ribbons and an entire military uniform, comprise a soldier's resume—a quick glance and the observer knows a good deal about the soldier.

There are also a variety of badges and crest pins which are worn on lapels, on epaulets, above the nameplate, or on either pocket flap or above a pocket. They indicate specialties, qualifications, and units in which the soldier has served.

While serving in the US Army, I received the following medals: The Bronze Star with two oak leaf clusters for Meritorious Service, The Air Medal with V device for Valor with two oak leaf clusters, the Air Medal with numeral 74, the Army Commendation Medal with two oak leaf clusters, the National Defense Service Medal, the US Vietnam Service Medal with one silver battle star, and the Vietnam Campaign Medal. I would also receive the Ohio National Guard service ribbon.

The numeral, 74, indicates I received seventy-four awards of the Air Medal. An aircrew member earned one Air Medal with every twenty-five combat flight hours, or every fifty direct combat support hours, or every one hundred general support flight hours.

I don't know how or who did the math, but we were told as soon as you crossed the wire you were in enemy territory—thus earning hours toward one more Air Medal. The single, silver battle star on my US Vietnam Service Medal indicates I took part in five campaigns.

I also received three, unit citations while serving with Bravo Company, 227. They included: The Army Valorous Unit Citation, the Republic of Vietnam Gallantry Cross Unit Citation, and the Republic of Vietnam Civic Action Honor Medal Unit Citation.

I earned the aforementioned unit citations while serving with Bravo Company, 227th AHB, so I wear the 227th Battalion crest above those ribbons.

My badges included Army Aviator wings and Sharp Shooter badge for the M-14. According to my records, I also received the Expert badge for the M-16 and the .45 caliber pistol. However, I did not earn those so I will not wear them. In fact, I never fired an M-16 until I got to Vietnam, and I couldn't hit a silhouette that stood eight yards away while firing a .45 pistol.

Concerning patches, I wore the following patches on my left shoulder, indicating I was serving with those units: US Army Aviation School (May 1969 through February 1970), 1st Cavalry Division, Airmobile (March 1970 until re-designation in June 1971), 1st Aviation Brigade (June to October 1971), 82nd Airborne Division (October 1971 to February 1972), Special Forces (February to August 1972), and again, the 1st Aviation Brigade (August 1972 to February 1973).

When I joined the Ohio National Guard, I wore the patch of the 107th Armored Cavalry Regiment on my left shoulder.

A soldier displays the patch of the unit he served with during combat tours of duty on the right shoulder. I can wear either the patch of the 1st Cav or the 1st Aviation Brigade. I always wear the Cav patch. I also wear four overseas bars on the right sleeve a few inches from its end. One bar represents six months of service, and my three tours of duty amounted to twenty-five months.

***

When the Army switched to its dress blue uniforms, unit badges, worn on the right chest pocket, below the flap, replaced shoulder patches.

Overseas Bars, worn above the left sleeve's cuff (Courtesy of the US Army).

No one returns unchanged! The true cost of war can only be measured by the toll it takes on the lives of our warriors. Being haunted by the sights, sounds and smells of war does not mean they are crazy. They are not weak or broken. We must recognize that this is a normal reaction to horrors no one should have to face. Understand and support our warriors.

—combatptsd.org

A college student said to the Vietnam vet, "Hey man, want to join my fraternity?"

The veteran replied, "I already belong to one."

"Yeah, which frat is that?" asked the college student.

"Mekong Delta," answered the vet.

—Vietnam Veteran humor

February 1973: Re-acclimation

I had heard stories about returning Vietnam vets damn near getting assaulted by long-haired, hippy peace creeps. No demonstrator ever spat at me, cursed me, or said anything derogatory. In fact, while flying home, a traveler in first class sent a drink to me, thanking me for my service.

However, I recall a less-than proper greeting at the local PLAV (Polish Legion of American Veterans). Still wearing my uniform, Dad and I dropped in a day or two after my return. The World War II vets there were indifferent to my presence—of that, I was certain. No one asked about Vietnam, my experiences there, or my opinions—no conversation of any significance took place. *Are you shitting me*? I wondered!

That was typical, and I found that indifference troublesome. I thought I would find camaraderie with veterans, all veterans. But, since many old-timers believed my generation of soldiers lost our war, Vietnam vets got the cold shoulder.

Now, I understand that approaching a veteran and wanting to talk about his time in the service can be tricky, especially with a combat vet. One should word the lead-in to such a conversation with, "Is it okay if I ask you about your experiences?" or "Do you mind talking about your service?"

Then, listen to the vet's response and how he delivers it. Most of the time you'll know whether to continue or to shut up. But at the PLAV and thereafter—nothing.

I put on my greens and went to my high school to pay the obligatory high school alum visit. The only person I remember talking to was Mr. Clarence Goterba, my junior-year American History teacher. Mr. Goterba is in the top three teachers I ever had. I loved his class, his enthusiasm, his patriotism—just about everything about him.

Mr. Goterba was genuinely excited to see me and had loads of questions about action, my medals, and what it was really like there, in particular, what our South Vietnamese allies were really like. I enjoyed talking with him and sharing information with him. Other teachers greeted me, but I honestly don't recall any other conversations of substance during the visit.

I visited the Civil Air Patrol meeting on a Wednesday evening and found things had changed considerably; fewer people, lack of enthusiasm—it just didn't feel right. My brother, Eddie, and his best friend, Bob Stanislaw, had left the squadron as well.

The Squadron Commander asked me to join as a senior member, but I declined. I knew the organization was in trouble and needed a good deal of help, but I was not willing to take up the cause of rebuilding CAP Squadron 301.

I would begin classes at Youngstown State University in the fall of 1973, so I immediately sought a decent-paying job to help cover the cost of impending tuition and living expenses. Packard Electric in Warren, Ohio, was hiring and veterans received preferential consideration—a gracious gesture. After completing the paperwork and the mandatory interview, they hired me on the spot.

The money was good and for six months I saved as much as I could, knowing I'd be quitting in September—the assembly line wasn't for me. Once muscle memory took over, my mind would detach itself and I was off on some mental journey, either profound or nonsensical. The hours passed more quickly that way and made the job just barely tolerable. I believe working on an assembly line could be termed legalized torture.

Steve and Eddie had the band going, and they welcomed me back. We got Johnny Pihonsky, one of Dad's cousins, to join as our sax man, thus adding another dimension to our sound. Within weeks, our newly named band, Sepesy Brothers and Memories, was playing steadily at weddings and parties.

I was a non-traditional student at YSU because I didn't attend college immediately after high school. Actually, at YSU, there were probably as many non-traditional students as traditional students.

When it was appropriate and the Ohio winters convened, I wore my field jacket, complete with all the US Army patches, which readily identified me as a Vietnam vet. It was no big deal, and no one ever commented on my veteran status.

Again, here at home, no one seemed to care, and no questions came my way. Since America had pulled out of Vietnam five months ago, people were now in a *forgetting* mode. I knew I'd never forget.

I can recall an encounter with an English professor. One day he was running his mouth about the war and I challenged him twice, respectfully presenting this prof, the only C in my four years at YSU.

Vietnam vets were given $180 a month. The state of Ohio kicked in a onetime payment of $500 that had to be applied to education.

The soldier is the Army. No Army is better than its soldiers. The Soldier is also a citizen. In fact, the highest obligation and privilege of citizenship is that of bearing arms for one's country.

—George S. Patton Jr.

29 July 1973 to 2 June 1974: Weekend Warrior

I joined the Ohio National Guard upon my separation from the US Army in Oakland. My assignment was to N Troop of the 107th Armored Cavalry Regiment, which flew Hueys and Cobras out of Canton-Akron Airport.

Sometimes the CO's comments confused me. The best example to illustrate this involved the bane of all guardsmen—haircuts.

"I know you guys are soldiers just two days out of the month," he said. "So, I won't worry about long hair. I do understand."

In reality, if a pilot wanted long hair, he would have to wear a short-hair wig, which is what I did. The wig looked terrible, but it covered my long hair and wearing it was hot and uncomfortable. Wearing a black Stetson helped the appearance a little, but the short-hair wig was not to the liking of the CO either.

The most excitement while with the 107 involved the nationwide truckers' strike in 1974. The state activated the 107 for eight days. Our mission was to demonstrate strength and to deter misbehavior by the strikers.

107TH Armored Cavalry Regiment shoulder patch of the Ohio National Guard (Courtesy of the US Army).

We flew our Hueys along the turnpike and Route 76 from Akron to Youngstown, then turned south and followed Route 7, south into Columbiana County. We were told to report any blockades to the Ohio State Patrol, but no one gave us frequencies for contacting them.

During those eight days, I amassed a staggering total of four flight hours. The rest of the time I hung out in the hangar with the other pilots, just killing time. After eight days of excruciating boredom, the strike ended, as well as the 107's mission. I returned to YSU, having missed one week of classes. The professors were understanding and cut me some slack.

One of N Troop's NCOs was John Twohig, who lived in Youngstown. John was active in Mahoning County veteran affairs and he had his act together.

There's an adage about NCOs—they are the soldiers that really run the Army. John personified that adage. John got a kick out of me, commenting about my youthful appearance, which he found to be amusing and unbelievable because of my three tours in Nam. He also openly wondered how I had accumulated over 2,500 hours in such a short time.

I could never figure something out: Aircraft were available for flight, but someone denied permission to fly them on some of our duty weekends. Then, while in formation we were told that some pilots were not meeting their monthly minimum flight requirements. Go figure.

Tuesday evenings were designated for night flying. If I wanted to fly, all I had to do was call the day before to make sure an aircraft was available. Night flying was enjoyable, especially on those smooth-as-glass nights that were so clear you could see forever. But more bullshit was just around the corner.

Bitching about some pilots not getting enough flight time continued. At the same time, night flying was becoming more and more restricted—birds were available, but for reasons not understood by me, we couldn't fly. I began to wonder, *is being in the Guard worth it?*

My favorite mission in the Guard occurred in the summer of '73—I buzzed the Sepesy house on Catalina Avenue. From a few hundred feet, I circled the family's house to get everyone's attention. Then, I did a high-overhead approach, screaming out of the sky and breaking about thirty feet above the roof—just like in Nam, but without a speed-reduction turn onto final approach to an LZ.

I climbed to altitude and watched everyone in the backyard checking out the idiot in the Huey who made so much noise that windows rattled. I wanted to land in the vacant parking lot across the street, but my co-pilot didn't want to get into trouble.

When I got home that evening, I stopped at the house to hear a ground's-eye-view report of my fly-by. Everyone enjoyed the brief air show. Eddie told me he opened the car door and started honking the horn—like I would hear it. My fly-by was important to me because Mom and Dad never saw my fly, So, for me, it was worth my illegal buzzing.

On another weekend I flew over Cedar Point amusement park and Put-in-Bay, I circled the park, then pressed onto the Commodore Perry Monument at Put-in-Bay, where I took some cool pictures.

I never took part in a summer camp because of timing. I reported for active duty after the 1973 summer camp and resigned from the guard before the 1974 summer camp.

During my time with the 107[th,] I managed one flight in an OH-58 and one in a Cobra. The unit's flight surgeon also saw that something was wrong with my posture, indicative of a back problem. He examined me and urged me to file a claim with the VA—which I did and the VA denied.

As the months went by, driving to and from Canton and Youngstown became a chore and offered plenty of time to think. *Was this hassle worth it?*

I recall asking the operations officer about getting more flight time. His answer made little sense—more bullshit.

So, on 2 June 1974, I put my black cavalry Stetson in its box, threw away my short-hair wig and left the Guard. My total flight time was 2,622 flight hours, sixty-six of which were logged during my ten months with the 107th.

***

After my departure from the Guard, I didn't see anyone from the 107, until thirty years later, when John Twohig's path and mine would cross again.

The air is the most mysterious, the most exciting, the most challenging of all the elements. We leave the planet, we leave the sea, we leave the earth. The air is no longer of this world.

—David Beaty, azquotes.com

Winter 1974: Poetry

I missed flying—the real flying I did with the Bravo Good Deal in Nam. At the risk of sounding morose, it saddened me, knowing I would never see such days again.

In an English class at YSU, the professor introduced several forms of poetry and for an assignment through which I was to reflect upon some personal feeling and write a poem. What I wrote follows.

Once We Flew

Once we flew, a machine and I, strangely allied by death. Oh, daring, insane joy!

Now, I amble, slowly—imprisoned by the now too familiar roads, our alliance destroyed by peace.

Oh, lonely, unholy sorrow.

—Masher 2-4

The professor thought it was strange that I would feel like I did about war. But she didn't understand—no one understands unless they've been there. She proved that when she said, "How morbid! Do you really feel this way?"

I'm sure she spoke those words—they cannot be deleted from my memory banks. I also recall the conversation continued for another minute. During that time, the professor's body language and facial expressions registered disgust. She was keen to end the conversation and leave the classroom.

Combat changes a person forever. Its effects stay with you forever. You don't forget things when somebody is trying to kill you.

** PTSD **

"Many veterans feel guilty because they lived while others died. Some feel ashamed because they didn't bring all their men home and wonder what they could have done differently to save them. When they get home, they wonder if there's something wrong with them because they find war repugnant but also thrilling. They hate it and miss it.

Many of their self-judgments go to extremes …. The self-condemnation can be crippling."

—David Brooks, "Moral Injury," *The New York Times*, 17 February 2015

6 January 1975: With infantry, armor, artillery and anti-aircraft assets, the North Vietnamese Army stepped up its general offensive. In III Corps, they attacked Bu Dop, Bu Gia Map (FSB Snuffy) and Song Be. In the Central Highlands, they attacked Ban Me Thout. All fell to the communists.

25 March 1975: The NVA's "Ho Chi Minh Campaign" begins with communist government orders that call for the liberation of the South, no later than 1 May, before the rainy season begins.

28 March 1975: With the fall of Hue, President Ford orders the US Navy to begin an evacuation of the South's coastal cities—chaos ensues.

1 April 1975: Lon Nol escapes from Cambodia. His government will surrender to the Khmer Rouge two weeks later. For the next three years, their reign of terror will cause two to four million Cambodian deaths.

7 April 1975: Over two-thirds of South Vietnam is now in Communist hands. Le Duc Tho, the north's "special advisor" to the Paris Peace accords, oversees his Army's offensive from his headquarters in Loc Ninh.

12 to 16 April 1975: The Lon Nol government of Cambodia surrendered to the Khmer Rouge, led by Pol Pot. During the next three years, the communists displaced, interred in work camps, tortured and slaughtered, between two and four million Cambodians. The communist invasion of South Vietnam continued.

25 April 1975: Avoiding possible coups, President Nguyen Van Thieu of South Vietnam flees his country.

29 April 1975: "Option IV" is initiated by US forces, beginning the helicopter evacuation of over 1,000 Americans and nearly 6,000 Vietnamese.

During the day on Monday, Washington time, the airport at Saigon came under persistent rocket as well as artillery fire and was effectively closed. The military situation in the area deteriorated rapidly. I therefore ordered the evacuation of all, American personnel remaining in South Vietnam.

—President Gerald Ford, 29 April 1975

30 April 1975: Saigon fell to the Peoples Republic of North Vietnam Army. South Vietnam's former capitol was renamed Ho Chi Minh City.

It is fatal to enter a war without the will to win it.

—General Douglas MacArthur

Early 1975: Prophesy Fulfilled

I spent a good deal of time watching the news from during the spring of 1975, when the North Vietnamese launched an all-out invasion of South Vietnam. I knew the Vietnam War was rapidly approaching its end.

So many places I knew were making headlines, all falling to the enemy forces, with little resistance mostly.

On 13 March 1975, Ban Me Thuot fell, followed by Kontum and Pleiku, and other familiar places including Dak To, the Mang Yang Pass and An Khe. Along the coast of the South China Sea, Da Nang and Hue fell, with Qui Nhon and Phan Rang following suit. In III Corps; Loc Ninh and An Loc, Quan Loi and Tay Ninh, Bu Gia

Map (FSB Snuffy) and Song Be, Xuan Loc ... and Phuoc Vinh, home of the Bravo Good Deal, yes Papa Vic, all fell to the enemy by mid-April

I tried to imagine what those places would look like, especially Phuoc Vinh—now overrun with enemy soldiers. I actually wondered what the NVA did to our structures ... to my hootch and the Red Hawk Inn.

Damn—the entire country collapsed!

During America's involvement in Indochina, 58,220 servicemen and women were killed; and 303,700 were wounded. (The last update occurred in 2008.)

The American soldiers were brave, but courage is not enough. David did not kill Goliath just because he was brave. He looked up at Goliath and realized that if he fought Goliath's way with a sword, Goliath would kill him. But if he picked up a rock and put it in his sling, he could hit Goliath in the head and knock Goliath down and kill him. David used his mind when he fought Goliath. So, did we Vietnamese when we had to fight the Americans.

—General Vo Nguyen Giap

War is politics for everyone but the warrior.

—Tiffany Madison, theysaidso.com

The Cost—US Army Aviation

The following information about rotary wing flight during the Vietnam War was gleaned from the Vietnam Helicopter Pilots Association.

During America's involvement in Indochina, 4,188 aviators died. US Army aviators that were killed in action numbered 1,869.

Helicopter pilots killed in action from age 19 through 22 numbered 773: 61 at age 19; 161 at age 20; 279 at age 21; and 272 at age 22.

Fourteen percent of the KIAs in Vietnam were officers. Of those officers, twenty-eight percent were helicopter pilots.

Over 40,000 helicopter pilots served in the Vietnam War. Of that number, 2,202 were killed.

1,205 warrant officers were killed while serving as US Army helicopter pilots.

Helicopter pilots killed in action numbered 649 in I Corps, 347 in II Corps, 516 in III Corps, 195 in IV Corps, 50 in Cambodia, and 77 in Laos.

Army Hueys compiled 7,531,955 flight hours in the Vietnam War between October 1966 and April 1975. The AH-1, Cobra, compiled 1,038,969 flight hours. It is the opinion of the VHPA researcher that the Huey and Cobra logged more combat hours than any other aircraft in the history of warfare.

During the Vietnam War, 11,827 helicopters served. Of that number, 5,086 were destroyed.

7,013 Hueys were flown during the Vietnam War. Of that number, 3,305 were destroyed; 1,074 Huey pilots were killed; and 1,103 crew members were killed.

Helicopters destroyed in the Vietnam War numbered 842 OH-6s, 270 Cobras, 132 Chinooks, 147 OH-13s, 93 OH-23s, and 45 OH-58s.

According to files at the National Archives, last updated on 29 April 2008:

US military casualties during the Vietnam War are: 58.220 KIAs; 304,704 WIAs and 2,338 MIAs. US Army KIAs numbered 38,224.

Other reports estimate total North Vietnamese and Viet Cong casualties as: 1,100,000 KIAs; and 600,000 WIAs. Total civilian casualties are estimated to be as high as: 2,000,000 for the South; and 2,000,000 for the North.

These figures change because of additional information coming to light.

World War II veterans received one-hundred percent of their tuition, room, and board—part of their GI Bill benefits. As a Vietnam vet attending Youngstown State University, the author received $175.00 per month and a onetime payment of $500 from the state of Ohio.

September 1973 through August 1977: Student, Youngstown State University— PTSD, Part 1

Big school or small school, Ivy League or state university—your education is what you make of it—despite bureaucratic bullshit, incompetence and stupidity, prejudice and vindictiveness. This assessment materialized, manifesting itself as hurdles for me to clear.

***

I had several confrontations with professors while a student at YSU. During the first week of an elective science class, the prof rambled on about his favorite television shows for half of the first two sessions. I got pissed off—*talk to me about science, not your goddamned TV shows*.

So, after the second class, I spoke to him, telling him as nicely as possible that I preferred to hear about science. He tried to laugh my comment off, but when he determined I was serious, he became visibly concerned.

After a couple more exchanges, he literally begged me not to go to his department chair to complain. Realizing I had scared the hell out of him, but still not trusting him; I took the simple way out—left the classroom, dropped the class, and didn't take my complaint to his boss.

During one of my first year's required courses, the prof would bad-mouth the military—I did not respond. But, after one too many slams, I offered a counterpoint, based on my experiences. My audacious comment caught him off guard. I vividly can recall his blush and a stammered response. You could hear a pin drop in the classroom. Long story, short—he gave me my only grade of C while in college.

I visibly angered an Asian professor during another elective course about Asian history. With my experiences in Southeast Asia, I thought I would enjoy the class, and enhance what I and observed about such cultures.

During one class, the professor's lecture turned to war. I asked an honest question, one whose answer would hopefully enlighten me. The question involved the value of human life in Asian cultures.

I was aware of acts of terrorism and butchery that went beyond *accepted* conduct during war. Also, recalling the barbaric treatment of allied prisoners of war during WW II and the Korean War, and kamikaze attacks on American ships, caused my wonderment. The professor denied the premise of my question and lectured me about my misperceptions.

His response surprised me. *Okay, I thought, I was tactful but still didn't get an answer.* I thought and somehow found words to ask a follow-up question.

He just waved me off and resumed his lecture.

After class I approached him to explain my reasoning for asking—that I did not mean to belittle or insult any aspect of any Asian culture, knowing I had not. The professor, still angered, refused to talk to me.

When I entered my junior year, I wanted to work on three majors and no minor simultaneously. That was contrary to the School of Education's policy—go figure.

The powers that be said, "No, two majors and one minor."

All right, here I go again—another confrontation I didn't need or want.

I called for appointments and met with profs, supervisors and the head of the department, wrote letters explaining my position, rationale, and desire. Eventually, they approved my plan.

My last example involves my first student-teaching experience, an elementary school assignment. My cooperating teacher did very little to assist me. She spent much of her time in the teachers' lounge or knitting at her desk, instead of guiding and assisting me—and this was the situation from day one.

Yep, you guessed it. I reported the situation to my supervising professor, pissed off the staff of the school in which I had been assigned, again drawing unwanted attention to myself. This time, the person in charge of assigning student-teaching positions reassigned me without delay.

I could cite more encounters—but these should suffice. But I should point out that I couldn't help thinking about parallel experiences in the Army during these many moments: meeting with the battalion commander after the near suicide mission with that Chickenman captain; nor the friendly fire episode with the major who didn't like my question about returning *friendly* fire; the death of Dao Tran, attitudes and incidents with Captain Botch and the 129th, and on, and on, and on …

Overall, my college endeavors were positive and rewarding. I graduated *magna cum laude* with a 3.64 GPA; was on the dean's list throughout my four years; was honored with membership in Phi Kappa Phi and Kappa Delta Pi, and received the Special Education Department's "Student of the Year" award; and I had three job offers as I was nearing graduation.

To provide more balance, most of my experiences with professors were positive. I recall those experiences with fondness and gratitude more than those that were negative or confrontational. However, after each negative episode, I asked why I had become embroiled in one confrontation after another? Why did I let things bother me to where I had to respond? What the hell was the matter with me?

** PTSD **

"How Can Anger After a Trauma Become a Problem?"

25

"In people with PTSD, their response to extreme threat can become 'stuck.' This may lead to responding to all stress in survival mode. If you have PTSD, you may be more likely to react to any stress with 'full activation.' You may react as if your life or self were threatened.

This automatic response of irritability and anger in those with PTSD can create serious problems in the workplace and in family life. It can also affect your feelings about yourself and your role in society."

—"How Can Anger After a Trauma Become a Problem?" from the US Department of Veterans Affairs; National Center for PTSD, 17 October 2019 ·

*When everything seems to be going against you, remember
that the airplane takes off against the wind, not with it.*

—Henry Ford

21 January 1977: A Slap in the Face

On 21 January 1977, President Jimmy Carter, wanting to heal the nation's wounds of the tumultuous 1960s and early 1970s, pardoned approximately 10,000 Vietnam-War-era draft dodgers. He also said that he would address upgrading discharges for approximately 100,000 deserters. To many Vietnam veterans and the families of WIAs, KIAs, MIAs and POWs Carter's action was a slap in the face.

Survivors of the war without the benefit of law degrees expressed their disdain and wondered if such action would be construed as a precedent that could justify future draft evasions and desertions. It is easy to understand that feelings of anger, disgust and betrayal were expressed by those veterans of all wars, not just Vietnam veterans.

This presidential action angered me and my mind immediately went to memories of my flight school buddies, Gary Plotz (WIA) and Butch Sears and Jeff Coffin, who were killed in action and the sacrifices they made for their country. I wondered how this action affected Butch's fiancé and family, and Jeff's family. And what about the oath that was taken by enlistees and draftees—that works both ways—for the government and those men and women who swore allegiance to the USA.

Perhaps the last line of the aforementioned article is the most impactful and profound: "Our country will have need of men and you will not be there."

** PTSD **"

Unlike simple stress, trauma changes your view of your life and yourself. It shatters your most basic assumptions about yourself and your world — 'Life is good,' I'm safe, People are kind, I can trust others, 'The future is likely to be good' — and replaces them with feelings like, 'The world is dangerous,' 'I can't win,' 'I can't trust other people,' or 'There's no hope.'"

—Mark Goulston, MD, *Post-Traumatic Stress for Dummies*, published by For Dummies, March 2012

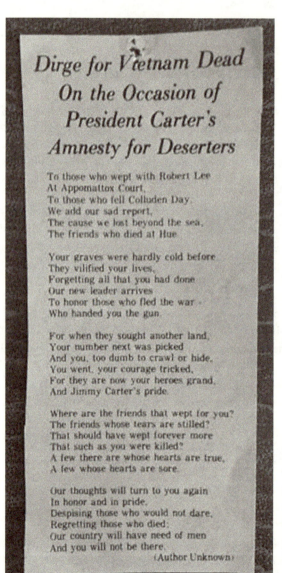

Dirge for Vietnam Dead On the Occasion of President Carter's Amnesty for Deserters

To those who wept with Robert Lee
At Appomattox Court,
To those who fell Colluden Day.
We add our sad report,
The cause we lost beyond the sea,
The friends who died at Hue

Your graves were hardly cold before
They vilified your lives,
Forgetting all that you had done
Our new leader arrives
To honor those who fled the war
Who handed you the gun

For when they sought another land,
Your number next was picked
And you, too dumb to crawl or hide,
You went, your courage tricked,
For they are now your heroes grand,
And Jimmy Carter's pride.

Where are the friends that wept for you?
The friends whose tears are stilled?
That should have wept forever more
That such as you were killed?
A few there are whose hearts are true,
A few whose hearts are sore

Our thoughts will turn to you again
In honor and in pride,
Despising those who would not dare,
Regretting those who died;
Our country will have need of men
And you will not be there.
                    (Author Unknown)

My Dad gave me this clipping and said, "More bullshit from more politicians! What's this country coming to?" Since that day, I kept the clipping pinned to my various bulletin boards. (Author's private collection).

I have often said that the lure of flying is the lure of beauty.
That the reason flyers fly, whether they know it or not, is
the aesthetic appeal of flying.

—Amelia Earhart

23 August 1977 to 16 August 1978: Flying in the Gulf of Mexico—PTSD, Part 2

In the summer, just before graduating from YSU, I received offers for two teaching jobs: one in Rockville, Maryland, the other in Ohio. However, the flight bug was biting at me and helicopter pilots were being hired to fly in the Gulf of Mexico. So, I flew to a Gulf state, for an interview with the international company. I was hired me so I put teaching on hold to experience offshore flying for at least one year.

My brother, Eddie, helped me move my things via truck to New Orleans where I had rented an apartment in Metairie, a suburb to the north of the Crescent City. My apartment was three blocks south of Lake Pontchartrain. After unloading my stuff, I bought Eddie a plane ticket and sent him home, while I prepared for at least one year of flights over the waters of the Gulf.

The company's newly hired pilots completed a one-week, refresher course. We reviewed basic helicopter systems and logged a few hours in the Bell 206 Jet Ranger (OH-58 in Army nomenclature). After a check-ride, I was ready for off-shore flight.

Living Conditions and Personnel

The company's chief pilot sent me to one of its bases which I will refer to as First Base. I would work seven days and be off for seven days. While on duty, I bunked in one of two long trailers with other pilots. I handled my own meals and could cook in the trailer or eat in nearby restaurants. The trailers were Spartan and thankfully, air-conditioned.

I learned early on to avoid one trailer because the immature element of the company was omni-present—pilots still acting as though they were flying in Nam, partying in the officers' club. Getting drunk after a day of flying seemed to be SOP (Standard Operating Procedure) for some company pilots.

One night, the lead pilot, who had cooked an enormous pot of spaghetti, sneaked up behind me and dumped the last load of pasta on my head. Such conduct would be a factor in deciding to remain a pilot or begin a career in education. After that incident, I stayed to myself much of the time and hit the bunk around nine o'clock.

During my year with the company, I encountered two pilots I knew from Vietnam. What were the odds? Both were sources of consternation, WO1 Pusilan and Captain Botch. Much to my dismay, the company hired both of them, but luckily, interaction with both lasted for only one week, and then both worked the shift opposite to mine.

Billions of mosquitoes, blood-sucking vermin inhabit the low-lying swamplands and coastal waterscapes that border the Gulf of Mexico. Many of the insects were large, about three quarters of an inch, and had striped bodies of brown and black.

In some remote areas, they attacked helicopters as soon as they landed. Before the rotor blades would stop turning, these insects would land throughout the cockpit and on one's body. I carried a can of repellant in my flight bag and applied it to my body several times a day. But some little bastards seemed to be impervious to such sprays and alit on exposed skin within seconds of landing.

Flight Conditions

My first off-shore flight occurred on 23 August 1977. I flew in a Bell 205 (the good old Huey) with the company's lead pilot for two-and-a-half hours. We headed south from First Base over the water and shot approaches to a couple of rigs, only twenty miles off-shore. I have to admit, my first flight off-shore was unnerving—all that water and no landmarks.

The primary concern about flying over water was an engine failure. If that occurred, I would land in the water on the helicopter's floats. Hopefully, the gulf's waters would be calm, and no sharks would investigate my arrival, and a rescue boat or helicopter would pick me up within a matter of minutes.

Landmarks were fewer than those used while flying over land. However, I would soon learn how my area of operation was divided into sections with the location of each rig or platform within a section clearly marked on its side. With experience, navigating within certain areas became commonplace as familiarity with each section grew.

Some Jet Rangers were equipped with ADFs (Automatic Direction Finders), beacons for homing to various rigs. But some birds had none. One day I had to fly to a lonely platform about one hundred miles offshore and my bird had no ADF! The only plus for that mission was that the day was unusually clear, which allowed me to seek a couple of distant rigs and use them as navigation landmarks. I had to hit my destination platform squarely or risk running out of fuel. Without an ADF I had to resort to dead-reckoning navigation, or time-distance-airspeed flying. I had to hold my heading, and adjust for the wind, maintain exact airspeed, and watch the minutes tick by, mile after watery mile. So, once I left the shore, I held a heading of southwest knowing that after an hour the platform should come into sight.

During the flight I altered my course ever-so slightly and flew by two other rigs. I read their locations (printed on their sides in large letters). I had figured the find factor correctly and had maintained the correct course. However, the further out, the expanse of deep blue water and the excruciatingly slow passage of time caused anxiety. And, for the last thirty minutes, there were no other rigs to serve as checkpoints.

About five minutes from my ETA (Estimated Time of Arrival) I spotted a tiny, tiny dot on the horizon, my platform I hoped. I nudged one of my passengers and pointed. "That should be it," I shouted over the noise of the engine. I dropped in altitude and buzzed the structure. Its location placard confirmed the destination. Happy and now at ease, I completed my approach and landed. My customers dismounted the bird and went about their business.

The platform was not bigger than a house, approximately forty feet by forty feet. Its construction was minimal with no amenities. Standing in one corner was its only feature, a small metal room with tools, pipes, and an assortment of spare parts. This shed served as the only feature of the platform's silhouette.

Typical off-shore production platform: note helipad at center. (Author's private collection).

I did not understand the platform's function, but it must have served some purpose in its isolated location, perhaps a capped wellhead that needed periodic inspection and maintenance. It was unmanned and its location was desolate, compared to the other rigs I had frequented.

My passengers were ready to leave about two hours later. I cranked up my refueled bird after another two hours, landed at my base. The return flight was enjoyable since I had topped off with fuel and *terra firma* was my destination.

I gathered experiences quickly, paying attention to the different rigs and their locations. And I studied my map, marking it appropriately with course lines and headings, and refueling stations. I quickly memorized headings and distances between significant points and learned the locations of the refueling stations. Navigation became second nature, much like cruising over the jungles of Vietnam.

Area of Operation

From August 1977 to April 1978, I flew out of one of First Base. On 20 April 1978, I transferred to Second Base, closer to my home on the south shore of Lake Pontchartrain, and I would be away from the negative influences of First Base.

While at the First Base, most of my missions took me south into the Gulf. Sometimes I would fly to helipad hubs to pick up or drop-off passengers.

Occasionally, I would fly into Moisant International Airport in New Orleans to ferry passengers to and from rigs. (In 2001, Moisant was renamed Louis Armstrong New Orleans International Airport.)

Flying out of Second Base was more relaxed, and the company's personnel were friendlier and more businesslike. And living in a hotel room at company expense was much nicer than the run-down trailers at First Base.

Weather

Learning the Gulf's sectors and prominent rigs was absolutely necessary to complete missions without getting lost, and without running out of fuel and being forced to pop floats to land on the water. Hazy conditions restricted visibility in this new environment and complicated the learning process. As a pilot, I had to search the sky constantly for other aircraft to avoid midair collisions. Hazy days guaranteed one thing—a monstrous headache and a physically and mentally depleted body wanting aspirin and sleep—nothing more.

Night flying wasn't fun. On 28 June 1978, I flew from Second Base to Grand Isle and off-shore to a rig in a Bell 212 (Huey). I had seen nothing so black, not even in Vietnam—blackness literally engulfed me and there was no differentiating the water from the sky. All things considered—we were flying IFR on instruments. We made it to the rig and returned without incident, but I vowed to never fly at night again.

One day while flying communications technicians around and landed to a rig in windy conditions; steady forty-knot winds with gusts to sixty knots. One tech, named Sheldon, dismounted and as soon as he did, my Bell Jet Ranger lifted itself off the deck. Sheldon immediately jumped onto the skid, his weight neutralizing the lifting power of the wind. I had experienced nothing like that before.

There I was, at flat pitch, and the power of the wind created enough lift to take my helicopter to a low hover while Sheldon was on the skids—amazing! I rolled back the throttle to flight-idle, which effectively decreased the rotor's RPMs, thus negating the lift effect of the wind. I told Sheldon it was unsafe to shut-down. He understood the circumstances and said he would be back in fifteen minutes,

"Just keep her running. When I get back, we'll head for home."

True to his word, Sheldon returned, jumped in and away we went, lifting off with incredible ease into the blistering wind.

One of the most pleasant weather days involved landing to a barge on water that was as smooth as glass, totally without ripples. This barge was about fifty miles offshore. It measured perhaps forty yards long and twenty yards wide. The water was so calm I felt no movement—a wonderful experience.

Contrarily, I had to land to a ship on a blustery day with seas easily over ten feet. Landing was difficult because of the wind's direction and the obstacles near the helipad—antenna and a crane's boom. I also had to time the landing so that I planted the bird at the top of the ship's rise and in a split second after making sure I was centered over the pad, lower the collective to flat pitch and ride the ship's constant rising and falling.

After one go-around, I dog-legged my final approach between the obstacles and planted my Bell Jet Ranger onto the pad. My customer dismounted, took his duffle bag from the rear seat, closed the door, and scooted away—but he forgot to secure the other door after grabbing this bag.

I yelled to him, but it was impossible to hear over the whine of the engine, turning of the rotors, and the blowing of the wind. Right then and there, I decided to hate that person. I attempted to reach the rear door several times, but it was impossible … and with every rise and fall of the ship, I was getting seasick.

My passenger had climbed into the control room at mid-ship where he was conversing with the ship's captain, oblivious to my dilemma. I tried to motion them, but they were having a good old-time bullshitting and didn't see me. I couldn't leave my seat, so I couldn't shut the bird down; the sea was too rough and wind too strong—

a dipping rotor blade could have severed the tail boom—and I was getting sicker by the second.

Five agonizing minutes passed. In desperation, I radioed the controller at Second Base. I asked the dispatcher to contact my customer via telephone and then radio—tell someone to come back to my helicopter to close the door—I was stuck.

Another brutal five minutes went by. Then I saw it—the captain reached for a radio and spoke into a microphone. I prayed my dispatcher had gotten through and relief was on the way—the last thing I needed was to vomit all over the cockpit.

The captain spoke to my forgetful passenger and pointed to me—another satisfying moment. A minute later, my passenger approached the helicopter, opened the door, and leaned inside. "What's the problem?" he asked.

"I can't take off with the door unlatched—it'll tear off in the wind!"

"I'll close it!" he yelled.

"Thank you! Secure it tightly!" I yelled, thinking, *you dumb ass*.

My passenger stepped back and closed the door. He locked it and then tested it, making sure it was indeed secure. He gave me a thumbs-up and left the helipad. Three seconds later I pulled pitch and escaped the grip of the roiling gulf waters. I continued to fight nausea and wanted to puke, but that sensation dissipated in a couple of minutes, only to be replaced by a mountainous headache.

When I landed at my base, the dispatcher wanted to know what had happened out there, so I related the complete story. After a few minutes, I excused myself and returned to my hotel room. Forget about eating—I took two aspirin and collapsed on the bed.

On 21 December 1977, a nasty storm was approaching from the southwestern waters of the Gulf and personnel had to be evacuated from many of the smaller rigs. It was the last day of my work-week and I had to fly four more horrendous hours to finish the mission. The wind was ridiculous—I needed a forty-five-degree crab to maintain my course.

The seas were rough with trailing white spray, ominously reminding me that this was no time for an engine failure. I remember looking down at the water before I landed during my final sortie—I decided to quit flying at that moment, but would tough it out until July, after only one year in the Gulf. I would begin looking for a teaching job on Monday.

Sea Life

There were plenty of sharks, huge sharks, and they were visible from my usual cruising altitude of two thousand feet. I usually cruised at two thousand feet, for safety's sake. I would also have more time to call a Mayday and my location if I went down.

The hammerhead sharks with their distinctive silhouettes were most clear. Manta rays were plentiful and cruised in great numbers, dozens and dozens of winged creatures just below the surface, gliding through the water with little effort.

Barracuda were also plentiful and congregated around the bases of rigs, scavenging food that was pitched over the side by galley hands. Many of these fish were over six feet long and could easily inflict a good deal of damage with their powerful jaws and needle-like teeth.

Emergencies

While flying Sheldon the commo tech, I experienced a hydraulics failure. I went through the emergency procedure and returned to First Base with no trouble. Compared to the three hydraulics failures I had in Hueys in Nam, flying the Bell Jet Ranger without hydraulic assistance was a breeze. I kept reassuring Sheldon we would land safely.

As I approached First Base, I simply shot a shallow-approach landing and greased the bird along through the grass, stopping as close as possible to my designated concrete pads. A relieved Sheldon thanked me. Unexpectedly, he made a big deal about my flying skills to the lead pilot—totally unnecessary, but appreciated.

I encountered no other mechanical problems or emergencies.

Passengers

Most passengers were well-behaved and appreciated being flown over the waters of the Gulf, the preferential mode of transportation over crew boats. They respected our skills as pilots and were usually glad to see us arrive to take them home after their shifts, especially when foul weather was approaching. Very few wanted to ride the small boats that also transported workers to and from rigs, especially in rough seas with swells over ten feet.

On one occasion I encountered a passenger who scared the hell out of me. He and two other passengers had readied themselves for departure. One sat next to me, and two more occupied in the rear seat. After briefing them, I cranked the bird and prepared for departure.

The trouble-maker, Mr. Big Mouth, was sitting behind me as I was backing up for take-off. Unbeknownst to him, I had already planned my departure from the enclosed pad and knew just how far I could back up before my tail rotor would strike a chain-linked fence.

I made a hover check, noting I was near maximum weight. I again cleared myself and began backing up. About three seconds later the Big Mouth screamed, "You're gonna hit the fence!" I mean, he *screamed* it!

I was so startled that I had to put the bird down and needed a few seconds to regain my composure. I was literally shaking and broke into a sweat—a most unusual reaction.

For a moment, I actually thought I had screwed up royally and nearly had a tail rotor strike. But I knew better. There was no reason for the passenger to have shouted. I had cleared myself and had remained clear but; he didn't know that. Nothing had changed in my landing area because I monitored my surroundings. I easily had sixty feet to maneuver for take-off. The only thing that could have happened was someone hopping the fence and approaching the bird from the rear—highly unlikely, and more so, very stupid. So, I was positive that I was clear for hovering and take-off.

But the passenger didn't shut his mouth—he added insult to injury by berating me, shouting, "What the hell's the matter with you?" and, "You wanna kill me?"

Now, the bastard had crossed the line. I shut down the bird while he continued to berate me and complain. "What kinda dumb-ass pilot are you?" I didn't respond to him, nor did I offer an explanation. But, when the blades stopped rotating, I dismounted the bird, opened the cargo compartment and told him to remove his gear. I told him, "I'm not flying you anywhere—you're unsafe."

He unleashed another current of obscenities and threats, but I restated my instructions and informed him that his presence jeopardized the safe operation of the aircraft. Begrudgingly, and with encouragement from one of the other passengers, Big Mouth and his buddy left while the third passenger, seated in the bird's front, remained on board.

I was well within my rights to remove the passenger because his behavior did interfere with the operation of the aircraft. He was indeed a safety hazard. I don't know where the guy went or what he did. But, to cover my ass, I reported the incident to the lead pilot at First Base upon my return, and nothing ever came of the incident. I suspect Mr. Big Mouth bummed a boat ride to his rig and continued to bad-mouth me.

The cooks on the rigs were great guys, and I got to know those on the platforms that I visited regularly. In the morning, they offered steak and eggs to my liking. At lunch, they offered steak and shrimp.

The cooks served shrimp all day long because the cooks could purchase it directly from the fishermen who would tie up along-side the rigs and sell the shrimp, fresh from the waters of the Gulf.

Departure

During my one year in the Gulf, I logged 562 hours, 305 of which were actually feet-wet, meaning off shore. My last flight was in mid-August 1978. I had already secured a teaching job so during the next week, I would travel to find an apartment. Two of my brothers, Eddie and Paul, joined me and helped me move.

I didn't miss the Gulf, its crazy weather, the headaches, many of the people and the scares.

"Real flight and dreams of flight go together. Both are part of the same movement. Not A before B, but all together."

—Thomas Pynchon, *Gravity's Rainbow,* Penguin Classics, 2006

"In our dreams we are able to fly … and that is a remembering of how we were meant to be."

—Madeleine L'Engle, *Walking on Water,* Convergent Books, October 11, 2016

Summer 1978: The Flyer-Philosopher

I met an interesting and enjoyable fellow while flying in the Gulf. He, too, was a former US Army warrant officer and helicopter pilot, with a tour of duty in Vietnam. His name was Hogan, which is an Indian term for a house. That's all I recall about him, save the following.

Hogan was part Native American and was in touch with nature and spirituality more than most people, including myself. One day our conversation drifted to childhood experiences. Hogan mentioned he, as a very young child, would fly over the land of his home—literally fly with no means of support or wings.

I found Hogan's remark fascinating, because of the vivid dreams I had when I was a child, flying over the neighborhood, especially over my family's yard and the adjacent field. Those flights seemed very real, but would eventually be forgotten or dismissed as just dreams—perhaps resolving them as the products of an overactive, five-year-old's imagination; a fascination with the story, *Peter Pan*; or maybe the simple manifestation of a burning desire to take to the sky. Who knew?

Hogan explained he had flown as a youngster, just as I had explained. Based on beliefs of native Americans, and their connections with nature and their Great Spirit, he was certain that he had flown. "It's real," he said. Hogan would then explain that as people grew older and learned more about themselves and their bodies, and about what could and could not be done based on physical limitations and established scientific paradigms, they negated, then dismissed what had been experienced as little kids, including such things as flying. They no longer believed such things occurred because they had come to know too much to the contrary. In short, they were told self-flight was not possible despite fading memories to the contrary—they accepted that fact, and therefore, never flew again.

Now, I'm a concrete sort of person—I have trouble with abstractions. So, is there some truth to Hogan's position? Are there things that are beyond our comprehension? Food for thought and a few follow-up conversations.

Hogan and I never conversed again. Within a few days, he moved on to another assignment or left the company, and we lost touch, but I will never forget his unique insight that precipitated one hell of an eye-opening conversation.

"Repeated trauma requires you to create a system of defenses that protects you. And these protections were so important. They saved your life. They protected your real self."

—Gretchen L. Schmelzer, PhD., *Journey through Trauma*, Avery, 2018

September 1978: Teaching—PTSD, Part 3

My first year of teaching was horrendous. I thought college had prepared me to teach kids that were classified as EMR (Educable Mentally Retarded). Unfortunately, that would not be the case.

The teaching materials were totally unacceptable. The textbook that was used by the previous year's teacher and what the administration expected me to use were for regular reading classes. A second set of textbooks were for psychology classes. Psychology classes for special ed students—that was absurd!

For EMR students, the teacher should teach survival skills—not theory or abstract concepts. I'd be teaching kids *supposedly* with IQs between fifty and eighty— the teaching of survival skills had to be employed. *They didn't call it Special Ed for nothing!* To get around the problem, I began writing and using my own programs that indeed addressed survival skills.

Student discipline was an enormous problem, improperly addressed by both teachers and administrators under the established Board of Education policies. Some teachers and administrators used a *laisez-faire* approach much of the time. Other times student misbehavior was down-played or ignored. And other times administrators considered questionable or *mitigating* circumstances, but still irrelevant to the incidents in question, concerning the unruly student.

Students that misbehaved were to be referred to the office by a teacher after completing a Disciplinary Referral Form (DRF). Board policies were clear about issuing a DRF. Policies spelled out specific infractions and their penalties. However, teachers, not wanting to call attention to themselves and fearful of reprisals, relaxed their reactions to disruptive behavior—they assumed the *real* company line and too frequently did not file DRFs.

By following Board policies, my number of DRFs increased, causing the administration to question my classroom management skills and overall abilities as a teacher.

My referrals were all legitimate, but the administrators danced around what they wanted a teacher to do—danced around what they should do in supporting the teacher—as a result, it became apparent to me that administrators frowned upon students with DRFs being sent to them, unless they involved severe violations of the student code of conduct.

During conferences with management, the administrator would raise the issue of my many DRFs. They did so cautiously by indicating that I should improve my classroom management skills—suggesting I write fewer DRFs.

They thought I was over-reacting—sometimes suggesting that I inflamed situations—indicating DRFs were to be the last option.

They said the number of my office referrals was extraordinary but didn't come out and say—knock it off with the DRFs!

I eventually determined the best way to explain my position was to cite Board policy, chapter and verse, and cite provisions in the collective bargaining agreement. To further cover my ass, I would also cite Board policy and contract language on individual DRFs. For example:

"I asked to see Johnny's pass that allowed him to report to class late. He replied, 'Kiss my ass, you, stupid mother f*****.' Johnny is in violation of Board Policy, Section IV, Paragraph 3, blah blah blah."

Employing such practices usually shut the administrator up or caused the conversation to move in another direction. I used management's own words against them.

But students caught on and adapted, resulting in the establishment of an unofficial and consequently ineffective norm. Students pretty well knew what they could get away with and knew that administrators were prone to issuing warnings or sending the student home early—something the student may have wanted, anyway.

As a result, students frequently directed vulgar and vile language toward teachers. Sometimes they made threats. "I know what car you drive," or "I know where you live."

And for the record, someone shattered the driver's window of my car moments after I arrived at home after school one Friday afternoon in early October. The following Monday, one punk approached me, grinning ear to ear, "You think you so bad, huh? I heard 'bout yo car. See? You f***in' with the wrong people!"

Attendance was another tremendous problem. Students frequently cut classes or the entire day. One Board policy stated that a student with five unexcused absences shall cause a grade of F. It was not uncommon for over half of my students to receive Fs for poor attendance.

Of course, such a percentage of failures caused concern in the administration. So, on some occasions, they changed my grades without my knowledge, thus reflecting a higher percentage of passing grades.

Sometimes administrators made changes without my knowledge because parents pitched a bitch and demanded a change—*or else*. *Or else* usually meant the threat of a lawsuit, petitioning the Board for action to change policies, involving a local civil-liberties group to raise a stink, or demanding the administration change their offspring's schedule.

After a horrible day at school, I would talk to other teachers. They were sympathetic, knew discipline was an immense problem, and knew most of the teachers didn't want to rock the boat or bring too much attention to themselves.

"That kind of thinking is why there are so many disciplinary problems," I'd respond. "Why the hell do we have rules and policies? The Board should be happy that a teacher is following them!"

As the year trudged on, I encountered student misconduct that was shocking. Consider:

On the first day of school, a student refused to quiet himself during morning announcements. He began pounding the back support of his Fiberglas seat—it broke in half. I wrote a DRF and handed it to the student.

"Man, they ain't gonna do shit!" he said, balled up the DRF and dropped it on the floor and walked out of the room.

I sent the DRF to an administrator who replied on the DRF, "Conference held." That amounted to a slap on the wrist.

During the Pledge of Allegiance, some students refused to stand, others stood with one foot on a desk, danced in place, talked loudly or cracked their gum, rummaged through purses, combed hair ...

I caught a kid selling marijuana in the stairwell. I escorted him to the office, handed the dope to an administrator and wrote a DRF.

The administrator responded by writing on the DRF, "3 nights detention in my office."

In the hall, a student dropped his pants and his underwear. He bent over, spread the cheeks of his buttock wide and shot the moon at two girls. I prepared a DRF.

The administrator responded, "Conference with student and called home."

An administrator asked teachers to check the restrooms more frequently for students that were smoking. Another teacher and I entered the boys' restroom—cigarette smoke had been drifting through the door into the hall. We told them to follow us to the office.

One responded, "Go f*** yourself 'cause I'm tired of you f***in' with me."

A student dropped a knife in front of me. I picked it up and filed a DRF.

The administrator did nothing of consequence.

A student was muttering at his desk, "F*** this," and "F*** that."

After a discussion with him in the hall, I returned him to his seat. The student exclaimed, "This is a bunch of cow shit! Hell! I'm eighteen. I couldn't care less!"

I wrote a DRF and handed it to the student. He yelled, "Kiss my left nut!"

An administrator responded on the DRF, "Held a conference."

A group of seniors had assembled in the school's parking lot, awaiting their Baccalaureate service to begin. They passed around a marijuana joint and posed for photos. They saw me through the window—laughed, waved, and gave me the finger.

I took issue with the administration's waffling approaches to policies. Consider the following positions and responses to disciplinary problems:

Some administrators favored some policies over others or were selective about what factors or evidence were to be considered. The administrator asked, "Are there any other witnesses ... I mean, other than yourself?"

Oh, I see, I thought, *are you thinking I dreamed all of this up—like I have nothing better to do.*

Some administrators presented creative interpretations of policies and decided accordingly by taking into consideration the personalities involved, past performances of the players, past decisions similar to the current issue ... bullshit, bullshit, bullshit.

Another administrative practice involved side-stepping or avoiding glaring problems.

In response to a brutal assault, I had witnessed an administrator said, "The situation you described is outside my parameters."

Hmm, I wondered, *your actions are contrary to established Board policy or filing charges?*

Regarding disciplinary issues or responding to DRFs I had submitted, some administrators practiced shifting the blame, as shown by the following response: ·

The administrator held the DRF in one hand and pointed at me. He snarled, "Listen! We've talked about your DRFs before," and then he walked away—end of discussion.

Some administrators rationed DRFs, telling teachers that downtown had run out of them—which was untrue.

Much of the time, parents were of little help, disrespectful when contacted on the phone about little Johnny, and infrequently or never attended teacher-parent conferences.

Some would take matters into their own hands and verbally assault a teacher. In one case, a parent physically assaulted in a hall. For that incident, the school refused to press charges, so I did, and the parent received a warning. *Hmm, open season on teachers was the message.*

Another time, four adult males rushed onto a school bus during dismissal in the school's parking lot. While three of the adults beat the hell out of one student, the other stood in the aisle blocking anyone that might interfere.

I ran onto the bus, climbed over the seats, going around the guy blocking the aisle, and was promptly punched on the side of my head, which dazed me. Satisfied with the punishment they had delivered the thugs ran away.

After the assault and information was gathered, not one administrator reacted positively about my intervention.

I asked an administrator if he would press charges and he said, "No."

I was pissed and let my demeanor show it. "No!" I said and feeling defiant, dared to ask, "Why?"

"Administrative prerogative," he said.

I left the meeting, went to the police station and pressed charges—victim's prerogative!

Later, the prosecutor dropped the charges for reasons that were never made clear to me.

I was beyond confused and still frustrated. *Is it really this bad*, I wondered, *or is it me? Was I stuck in some Twilight Zone of public education? This can't be real.*

But answers and validation of my position and clarity of perceptions would be forthcoming. Proof would come from the most unlikely of sources—but not until the last week and the last day of school

"Everyone has thoughts or beliefs that help them understand and make sense of their surroundings. After trauma, a person with PTSD may think or believe that threat is all around, even when this is not true. He or she may not be fully aware of these thoughts and beliefs. For example, a combat Veteran may become angry when his wife, children, or coworkers don't 'follow the rules.' He doesn't realize that his strong belief is actually related to how important it was for him to follow rules during the war in order to prevent deaths.

If you have PTSD, you may not be aware of how your thoughts and beliefs have been affected by trauma. For instance, since the trauma you may feel a greater need to control your surroundings. This may lead you to act inflexibly toward others. Your actions then provoke others into becoming hostile towards you. Their hostile behavior then feeds into and reinforces your beliefs about others. Some common thoughts of people with PTSD are:

'You can't trust anyone.'

'If I got out of control, it would be horrible, life-threatening, or could not be tolerated.'

'After all I've been through, I deserve to be treated better than this.'

'Others are out to get me,' or 'They won't protect me.'"

—Cy Mulholland, *A Marne Mind, A Soldier's War with Recovery*, WestBow Press, January 2012

"Because of dissociation, many victims are able to remember the abuse only when a certain object, smell, color, scene, or experience triggers a sudden, severe reaction. During a flashback one seems to see, feel, hear, smell, or taste something from the past as if it were actually happening in the present. In a visual flashback, you actually see the scene of your abuse, or you may see an object or image that reminds you or is symbolic of your abuse."

—Beverly Engel M.F.C.C., *The Right to Innocence*, An Ivy Book, Random House Publishing Group, 1989

October 1978: Ducking for Cover—PTSD, Part 4

I was walking to parking-lot duty when I stopped by the cafeteria duty to chat with a fellow teacher, Mike. There were about four hundred students in this huge room, and the noise was considerable. Students were talking loudly, there was some shouting and laughter. The students sat at eight-foot tables with standard folding metal chairs. Mike and I were engaged in conversation.

BANG!

I immediately crouched down and covered my head with my arms. Three or four seconds later, I realized where I was and deduced the noise was not a harbinger of death such as in-coming rockets.

I rose to my feet and looked at Mike, who was smiling. "What the hell?" he said as dozens of nearby students pointed at me and howled with laughter.

I blushed, literally feeling the temperature rise over my face and neck. I didn't know what was worse, the noise I had just heard or the students responding with heckling and laughter. But I did my best to ignore the embarrassment and gathered my composure.

"You, okay?" asked Mike.

"Oh, yeah, now that hasn't happened in a while."

"Flashback?"

"I think so—loud noises like that … they still get to me."

"You wanna talk?"

"Not now—I've got to get to the parking lot. But later on, sure, I can tell you a couple of stories."

As I stepped toward the door, I heard one or two wise-ass comments from one or two wise-ass students. In the relative quiet of the hallway a student looked at me, "Are you okay?" she asked.

"Just fine, now, thank you for asking," and kept on walking.

The young lady stayed at my side and said, "I've seen my brother do the same thing. Were you in the war?"

"Yes, I was, young lady. Is your brother, okay?"

"Uh huh, but sometimes noises scare him."

I held the door for the young lady and we both walked into the parking lot. She went on her way, and I positioned myself near the entrance. "Thanks for asking," I said.

"You're welcome," she responded and walked to her car.

After school, Mike and I went to a local seafood restaurant. During our supper, I answered all of Mike's questions about my tours of duty in Vietnam.

** PTSD **

"Hyperacusis and PTSD"

50

"Those with Post-Traumatic Stress Disorder (PTSD) can often develop difficulties with sounds such as an exaggerated startle response, fear of sound (phonophobia), aversion to specific sounds (misophonia), and a difficulty in tolerance and volume of sounds that would not be loud by normal hearing individuals (hyperacusis)…"

—PTSD UK, 2020

I find some common sounds to be annoying, even nerve-racking, much more than they should be. Low-pitched hums and background noises can be most agitating and distracting, such as the running of a vacuum cleaner or clothes dryer, the whirring of a fan. But, the most disturbing, indeed frightening noises that shock my body and cause be to cover my head, need not be very loud—unexpected noises cause me to react in the same way.

I once sat at a table and heard a thump—a small, empty, plastic container fell onto a counter top. I cringed and shivered for just a few seconds. The noise was not loud at all, but I reacted as if someone had loudly slammed a door shut.

This conversation about hyperacusis is continued with more profound examples in chapters: "October 1978: Ducking for Cover—PTSD, Part 4" and "1970 ad Infinitum: Some Things Will Always Be the Same—PTSD, Part 24."

1 May 1975: The new Provisional Revolutionary Government of Vietnam banned acting like Americans.

Winter 1981: Return to Active Duty ... but only Briefly

I received a letter from the Department of the Army—it was looking for former pilots who would go on active duty for up to three months to become proficient in helicopters again. Any pilot who entered this program would be placed on an inactive call-up list, and in the event of a national emergency would be called to active duty before reserve and guard units.

I considered this *if-you-then-you* proposal and after very little thought agreed to six weeks of active duty. The school year had been a rough one with a long strike. The extra money would come in handy.

I called the phone mentioned in the letter and spoke with an officer about an assignment and he said I could go just about anywhere I wanted, east of the Mississippi River. I considered Fort Knox and Fort Campbell, both in Kentucky. Then, I thought about Fort Devens, in Massachusetts. I had never been to New England and thought I'd like to see the region.

Fort Devens was located a little east of dead center Massachusetts, about thirty miles west of Boston. The twelve-hour drive from home was irrelevant, so I decided on Fort Devens, which was immediately approved by the Army.

So, on 23 July 1981, I shaved off my beard and got a haircut. The next day I drove to Devens and reported for duty to a unit whose designation I can't recall. I was issued new flight gear and told to study for a written flight exam, which I passed two days later.

On 27 July 1981, I flew in a Huey for the first time since 1974. My feel for the aircraft and control touch returned within that first flight. But I also knew I was nowhere near as proficient as I had been in Vietnam.

During the next six weeks, I would only fly eight days and log a mere seventeen hours. I'd like to say, "Wow," but there was no wow—the thrill was gone.

Pleasant moments of this assignment were few. I flew over Plymouth Rock, in and out of Logan Field in Boston and Martha's Vineyard, and cruised over the Kennedy Compound in Hyannis Port. The periwinkle heather from altitude was spectacular.

However, some commanders resented guys like me—we were taking flight hours away from the regular guys assigned to their unit. And for that reason, my CO didn't appreciate my presence, making that apparent the first time our paths crossed, when he pounced on me in the operations room.

I was standing in front of the counter in the operations room waiting for my AC and briefing. One of the senior commissioned officers had just entered and approached the counter. A few seconds later I said to my AC, "Well, time to go bore holes in the sky," a common aviation expression meaning, let's go fly.

The senior officer immediately jumped in my shit. "You're one of those inactive guys, aren't you?" he spouted.

"Yes, Sir."

He then told me how he did not appreciate my comment about boring holes in the sky, nor did it reflect professionalism. He ranted and raved for a good two minutes, during which he probably explained why I was unprofessional among many other things that were troubling him that morning.

When given the opportunity to respond, I told him that the comment was nothing more than another way of saying; we have our mission, so let's go. And it was a common expression spoken in Vietnam.

But the senior officer didn't want to hear it and berated me further in front of at least six other soldiers.

So, I stood there taking the unwarranted scolding and lecturing while I turned several shades of red, reflecting embarrassment through anger.

The only other comment I can remember making was to explain how the Army invited me into the program, which is why I was in his unit. But it didn't matter what I said.

I figured this officer was pissed at the Army and its program, and I was a convenient target for venting his frustration. So, I stood there and took it, just like enduring bullshit from TAC officers during flight school, while thinking about a way to jab back.

"Is that all, Sir?" I dared to ask during a break in his ass-chewing—the only way to register defiance.

"That's all, Mister! Get out of here …blah, blah, blah."

So, I immediately turned and walked away while his mouth continued—my second display of defiance. I heard him say something about how guys like me were using valuable blade time, that his active-duty pilots should have received.

After that encounter, I flew very little.

So, I would report for morning formation every day. As the company proceeded to physical training, I went to the operations desk to check the day's schedule of missions. If I had not been scheduled, I would say, "I'll be at my hotel. You have my number. If you need me to fly, just call and I'll be here in twenty minutes."

I spent a lot of time in my room, preparing units of instruction for my special-education classes, and literally wrote two years of English lessons, which I called my *Survival Words* units. I resigned myself that I wouldn't be flying, so I made the best of the time and still cleared about two thousand dollars. But, as I mentioned earlier, the thrill was gone, and I'd never fly again.

***

A Breakdown of my 3,205 Flight Hours, June 1969 to August 1981:

Flight School: 216 hours, including instrument training in an OH-13 and transition to the UH-1.

Vietnam: 2,200 combat flight hours.

Stateside Duty: 227 hours.

Total Military Time (OH-23, OH-13, UH-1, OH-6, OH-58, AH-1): 2,643 hours.

Civilian Flight Time: 562 hours, including 305 offshore.

Total: 3,205 flight hours.

Joey

You are not broken and in need of fixing. You are wounded and in need of healing.

—Danu Morrigan, goodreads.com

Winter 1982: Post-Traumatic Stress Disorder, Part 5

During World War I it was shell shock, and during World War II it was battle fatigue. After the Vietnam War, a new term, Post-Traumatic Stress Disorder or PTSD confronted a new generation of veterans.

PTSD is a mental condition that affects any person who has experienced a traumatic event. It is not exclusive to combat veterans. It manifests itself in myriad ways which complicates the veteran's ability to cope with everyday situations.

***

In 1973, while watching the return of American POWs from North Vietnam, after the cease-fire. I remember trembling and without success, trying not to cry while watching the very moving scenes of American servicemen being reunited with their families.

Afterwards, I didn't give my reaction to the homecoming much thought and life went on. But, on 13 November 1982, the Vietnam War Memorial, "The Wall", was dedicated in Washington DC. I watched the ceremony and activities on TV and again, crying considerably. I was suffering from PTSD (Post-Traumatic Stress Disorder) and didn't know it.

A few months later, while at a mall, I walked by a veterans' display that explained the plight of Americans still being held as prisoners by the North. I picked up a pamphlet about PTSD and saw that I fit the condition's profile by identifying several symptoms that I had experienced. I was also serving as an official of my teachers' union and was under a great deal of pressure. So, I contacted the VA, and a representative steered to its veterans' out-reach program.

My first meeting was mostly organizational and procedural. I met with a psychologist who took background information, explained his role and approach and what I could expect, and then set up counseling sessions. I was comfortable with him, but the rest of the environment rested uneasily with me.

A group of about ten Vietnam vets hung out in the building, playing pool in the lounge, drinking beer and eating snacks. Their appearance was that of the stereotypical Vietnam Vet, disheveled and alienated from society. They were boisterous, smoked, and nursed cans of beer.

I was never comfortable with such groups, and this collection of misfits made for no exception. One vet was a captain that smoked one cigarette after another. He wore an old beat-up field jacket with patches and captain's bars. The other vet that stood out was an obese guy who was also never without a can of beer and a cigarette. He talked, joked, and laughed incessantly. I'll call them Captain Jacket and Brewski.

Upon arriving for my counseling sessions, Captain Jacket or Brewski would offer me a beer and start bullshitting. They would make many meaningless comments or jokes about their buddies and themselves. Because of this assault, I had no time to gather my thoughts for my upcoming session with the psychologist.

The lounge and waiting area were one, and the same, so I could not avoid the group. Not wanting to interact with them, I waited in my car the next time I arrived. There, I could prepare my thoughts and enter the building a minute or two before my appointment. It was pure relief when the psychologist opened his door and called my name.

The first session was emotional, and I broke down. The psychologist said he wanted me to discover my personal My Lai (pronounced me lie) incident, or trauma, and confront it. My Lai, where Lieutenant Calley and some of his soldiers slaughtered over four hundred innocent Vietnamese civilians, caused many of Calley's men to develop PTSD—hence the connection.

I recalled events already described in this memoir, but the primary focus was on the death of Dao Tran, my My Lai, which occurred on the flare mission of 8 July 1970. I had been carrying around and suppressing the guilt from that incident for thirteen years. Other incidents added to the disorder: the headless corpse, and the young soldier dying on board my Huey in the arms of Colonel Galvin were just two.

After two more sessions, the psychologist asked if I wanted to continue.

I thought that was strange. Shouldn't he be advising me about the duration of sessions? Not knowing any better and not liking the environment, I decided not to continue. I thought I had confronted my demons and was a changed person. He also asked me to join his group counseling session with the crew of vets that congregated in the building's lounge. I declined.

I took two things with me from this brief experience: a veteran had to identify his own personal My Lai, his demon, his trauma, and confront it. The other thought: I should understand that war was the most irrational act of mankind and cannot be explained or understood from a rational point of view.

***

This short-lived experience was valuable, and I got a glimpse of how the war had affected me—but just a glimpse. I did not know that this outreach program was the VA's first and ineffective attempt in dealing with Vietnam vets suffering from PTSD (Post-Traumatic Stress Disorder). I had thought I had become a changed person during that experience and was very wrong.

** PTSD **

"Why Get Treatment"

"The decision to get care for PTSD symptoms can be difficult. You are not alone if you feel nervous. It is not uncommon for people with mental health conditions like PTSD to want to avoid talking about it. But getting help for your symptoms is the best thing you can do…

…You don't need to let PTSD get in the way of your enjoyment of life, hurt your relationships, or cause problems at work or school."

—"Why Get Treatment?" from by US Department of Veterans Affairs; National Center for PTSD, 7 August 2020

12 to 14 May 1975: America's last action in Indochina occurred with the taking of the US ship Mayaguez by the Khmer Rouge. In response, US Marines attacked Tang Island and suffered 38 KIAs, 50 WIAs, and 3 MIAs. During the battle, the communists released the crew and ship. The casualties of this battle were the last suffered by America during the Vietnam era.

Spring 1983: A Local Parade

The Market Street Bridge had been closed for nearly two years, being replaced by a new span. In April 1983, it was ready for dedication and renamed the Vietnam Veterans Memorial Bridge. The organizers invited all Vietnam vets to attend the event, which included marching in a parade.

The veterans assembled by the old Sears building on Market Street. I was one of approximately sixty veterans. I wore my Army green jacket with ribbons and patches, and Cav hat. The first guys I recognized were Captain Jacket and Brewski. and others from the VA Outreach Program. I didn't know anyone else.

Much to my chagrin but true to form, they approached me and began bullshitting. But, within a minute or two, the parade's organizer, holding a clipboard, approached us. "Who's in charge?"

My enthusiasm about the impending parade quickly sank. I thought, *this guy is the organizer, and he's asking, who's in charge? Doesn't he know?*

Brewski pointed to me and said, "Well, we have an officer right here. I guess he's in charge."

I said, "Wait a minute," I said, "here's a captain," pointing to Captain Jacket.

Everyone burst out laughing. "He's no captain," said Brewski.

"What? He's wearing captain's bars."

Captain Jacket stopped laughing and said, "This jacket fits just right, so I wear it. I ain't no captain."

That stunned me, angered me a bit, but I managed a smile. This idiot was impersonating an officer, and that didn't sit right with me. I let it go, not wanting to keep interacting with assholes to a minimum.

The organizer turned to me, "Well, it looks like you're in charge. Here's what I want you to do." Reluctantly, I listened.

The organizer explained we should form up and march down the center of Market Street, right on the yellow line. We were to stay a few paces behind the marching band and salute at the bottom of the bridge when we passed the reviewing stand.

I didn't want to be in this position, didn't want to lead this ragtag bunch of stereotypes. I wanted to be in the formation with everyone else—just another vet.

"Any questions?" asked the organizer.

Still reluctant, I replied, "I guess that's simple enough."

"Good," he said, "get 'em formed up here. When the band moves, you move."

"Okay," I said.

We fell in with me calling out orders that were still all too familiar; dress right, dress; ready front; dress front dress; and ready front again.

"At ease, men," I said, and taking charge surged through me, just like leading a flight of Hueys. "Men, this is our day. Today we own this street and that new bridge. We are finally being welcomed home *by* our home. So, let's show pride and savor the moment so you can recall it later in life. Look sharp and be proud of who you are, a Vietnam veteran."

I know this might sound crazy, but I actually saw a transformation come over this eclectic collection of veterans. They adjusted their hats and jackets, smiled and nodded. They appeared to feel good about themselves and being *here*, in a long overdue but special moment.

"Any questions?" I asked.

There were none, so I said, "I need an NCO."

Of all people, Captain Jacket stepped forward, "I was a buck sergeant—really, I was."

"Roger that, Sergeant, you take up the rear and keep the men in line. I'll be at the front of the formation."

"Okay, Sir."

Wow, I thought, *he called me, Sir.*

Within seconds, the band started playing and stepped off down Market Street.

"Atten-hut!" I called. "Right face!" My formation turned to the north, and I took my place in front of it. "Forward, march!" And away we went.

For the next thirty minutes, we marched down Market Street. Few people stood by to watch, but those who did cheered and applauded us. I felt good. I suspect all of us felt good.

We crossed the newly named Vietnam Veterans Memorial Bridge. The American flag flapped in a steady breeze on this cool spring day.

"Eyes ... left," I shouted and saluted the flag. "Ready ... front!" I shouted, and we continued our way to the reviewing stand at the base of the bridge in front of the courthouse's main entrance.

The grand marshal of the parade was a local man, retired Air Force general, Chester Amedia. Instead of just marching by as instructed by the organizer, I brought my company to a halt in front of the reviewing stand.

"Left face!" I shouted. I then proceeded to the center of the formation, faced the stand, and called, "Present ... arms!"

Everyone saluted.

After General Amedia returned our salute, I called, "Order ... arms! Right ... face!"

I returned to the head of the formation and called, "Forward ... march!" and led the rag-tag band of brothers toward the square where the parade units stopped and dispersed.

We Vietnam veterans had finally realized our long-awaited welcome-home. We milled around for a while and bummed rides back to our cars.

All things considered—it had been a good day.

3 December 1975: Now in control of Laos, the communist Pathet Lao established the Peoples Democratic Republic of Laos.

20 December 1975: Approximately 140,000 South Vietnamese refugees had been processed for resettlement in the USA.

1984 and 1986

On 23 April 1984, I married a beautiful woman who taught in the same school system as I did. This marriage would be her second, and it came with her ten-year-old son.

***

While teaching, I would sometimes field questions about the military and my service. For the first few years I would answer such questions tersely, revealing very little about my experiences and not wanting to drift away from the lesson at hand. And I had already learned that such extra involvement soured quickly.

For example, I once took in a videotape about the holocaust as a reinforcement activity for a social studies lesson. The kids ridiculed and laughed at the most graphic scenes of the concentration camps. I know such responses were because of immaturity, but the extent of their amusement and then disinterest bothered me. So, I swore off repeating such activities.

However, during the next few years questions about the military and my service became more frequent. Again, I would answer them as tersely as possible but also reconsidered a mini-lesson about my Vietnam experiences.

So, for the next two years, I took slides and war memorabilia to class to conduct a one-day, show-and-tell lesson about the Army and the war in Vietnam, on Veterans Day in November. The kids weren't especially interested, so after the second year I was already considering curtailing the activity. The decision to stop came easier than expected when someone stole some pictures and pieces of shrapnel I had placed on my desk. Some little son of a bitch stole them—so never again!

***

During 1983, my feet began to tingle and fall asleep while I would walk, sit, and even drive. I was also experiencing substantial pain in the lower back that radiated through my hips and down the legs—classic symptoms of disc trouble.

In early October, after consulting with three doctors, I decided that surgery was the way to go. After a four-hour operation, nurses and orderlies moved me onto my bed. But my feet were hanging over the edge of the mattress, causing considerable pain. Instead of placing pillows under my feet, two nurses raised me to a near-sitting position and pulled me toward the head of the bed. My heels caught on the edge of the mattress and I exploded in pain so intense and beyond description that I screamed, shocking my wife and Mom. They had dislodged the bone splints that the surgeons had positioned between my vertebrae.

The next day, one of the same nurses that had pulled me across the bed, forced me to stand, causing me to become paralyzed from the waist down for a few minutes. That nurse told Mom that standing was the usual procedure on the day following surgery and that I was, "Acting like a baby."

Five days later, corrective surgery took place. The bone splints inserted during the first operation had indeed been dislodged and nerve damage had occurred. This time the surgeons implanted a titanium device to fuse vertebrae L-4 and L-5.

My life changed dramatically after that stay in the hospital; I cannot stand on my toes, and I have lost significant strength in my legs, developed foot-drop and balance problems.

***

One of the best days in my life was 29 April 1986—my beautiful daughter, Jacqueline Noelle, was born. She was a gorgeous baby with blue eyes and red hair. As she grew, she resembled Mom more and more.

65

"There are wounds that never show on the body, that are deeper and more hurtful than anything that bleeds. Don't wait until you break."

—Laurell K. Hamilton, *Mistral's Kiss*, Ballantine Books, 2006

Summer, 1985: The Wall—PTSD, Part 6

In the summer of 1985, my wife and I visited Washington DC. We visited "The Wall", the Vietnam War Memorial at the west end of the mall, next to the Lincoln Memorial.

As we traveled to DC, I thought a great deal about how I would conduct myself at the wall. I recalled my reaction when the POWs returned, my sessions with the VA's Outreach Program, and thought the visit might provoke an emotional response. That worried me, but determined to complete the pilgrimage.

We approached the Wall, following the brick pathway as it sloped a few feet below street level. A registry, listing the names of the 58,000-plus soldiers who died in Vietnam, rested on a podium-like stand a few feet before the first and lowest of the wall's black granite panels. Next to each name on the registry were the numbers of the panel and line where that name could be located. I stood before the registry and started leafing through the pages, looking for Butch Sears and Jeff Coffin, two flight-school classmates, killed in action in November 1970.

My right hand began to tremble, then shake, literally. It shook on its own accord and wouldn't stop. My left hand followed suit and within seconds my entire body trembled. I shook so intensely that my sunglasses fell from my face, and then I burst into tears, wailing out of control.

I could not stop this unexpected breakdown of both body and mind. An Army officer close by, picked up my glasses and said something to console me, and my wife put her arm around me. She tried to console me also but truly didn't know what to say; such was the suddenness and intensity of the moment. She too cried.

We eased our way from the entranceway to a shady area, me still out of control, incapable of rational thought and action—completely vulnerable, like nothing I had ever experienced. I cried for fifteen or twenty minutes, and then the trembling eased.

After settling further, I realized how pleasant the setting was. Sitting on the thick green grass was soothing and a gentle breeze cooled my body. But I had to complete this, my final mission. We went back to the registry, and I copied the location information for Butch and Jeff—this time without breaking down, although tears still streamed from my eyes.

As we walked along the walkway, descending ever so slightly past the names and our ever-present reflections, I realized some things about the wall that were absolutely true: its simplicity was magnificent and its design, positive. I had become part of it. I was back in Nam, but still at home. Its quiet dignity drew me in and comforted me as if I were being embraced by the spirits of the fallen. It returned me and welcomed me to that defining part of my life that was irrefutably the most important aspect of my being.

As we drifted along, emotions overpowered me again. I cried more and more but remained in control of myself. I found the panel and then the lines for Butch and Jeff. They died three weeks apart in November 1970. *Fitting,* I thought. *They occupied the same panel—close during flight school, close in death ... and in memoriam.*

I touched their names, moving my fingers across the letters of Gordon B. Sears, and Jeffrey A. Coffin. I thought about the one picture I had of Jeff and me, on an old ship in Savannah. I thought about Butch and the only picture I had of him, our class picture that was taken on the day we received our wings and bars, and also recalled that Jeff was missing from that class picture.

I recalled rooming with Butch and meeting his fiancée, the typical blonde beauty from California. I thought about Butch begging to let him drive my Ford Maverick to the PX after being told to let no one borrow my car. But I gave in to his pleadings and gave him the keys. Butch returned minutes later without incident and a candy bar for me.

I thought about how quiet Jeff was—but a warrior and an outstanding pilot. I recalled sharing chocolate chip cookies with him and other classmates, cookies Mom had sent. I thought about many things.

The visit to the Wall exhausted me, for the rest of the evening did no more. I wondered, *was this visit, this reaction, my final mission—or would there be more?*

During my three tours of duty, I served in five campaigns:

Winter-Spring 1970: 1 November 1969 to 30 April 1970;

Sanctuary Counteroffensive: 1 May 1970 to 30 June 1970;

Counteroffensive Phase IV: 1 July 1970 to 30 June 1971;

Consolidation I: 1 July 1971 to 30 November 1971;

Cease-Fire: 30 March 1972 to 28 January 1973.

> Some Americans continue to serve unnamed campaign after unnamed campaign, those of imprisonment, torture and survival, as POWs of the North Vietnamese and in other communist and former communist countries.

America without her soldiers would be like God without His angels.

—Claudia Pemberton, allauthor.com

25 December 1985: Honorable Discharge

The date on the document was 25 December 1985 and totally unexpected—my honorable discharge from the Army arrived a day or two after Christmas. Since I had been an officer and a highly trained helicopter pilot whom the government had invested thousands of dollars in training, the Army had kept me on their inactive role.

I had been subject to call-up if the US would have gone to war and needed every former able-bodied soldier. Just how able-bodied I would have been and being able to pass a flight physical because of my back and its titanium implant was questionable. I know I could have flown again, and honestly, and if needed—I would have gone.

Today, for the first time since 12 December 1968, I was no longer obligated to serve in the US Army.

From early inspirations to honorable discharge, wearing the silver wings of a US Army aviator, being an American eagle was an honor. I'd serve again. (Wikimedia Commons, Join the Army Air Service, Be an American Eagle, Charles Livingston Bull, Alpha Litho. Co., Inc., N.Y. 1917 (Public domain).

Trauma is hell on earth. Trauma resolved is a gift from the gods.

—Peter A. Levine, azquotes.com

1988: Demon Dreams—PTSD, Part 7

In 1988, I started having nightmares, most of which involved helicopters and Vietnam. I do not know what caused their sudden and disturbing appearance.

The wire dream repeated itself. I would fly in a Huey and high-tension wires would appear. To avoid them, I would simply climb over them. But then, more wires would suddenly stretch in front of me, layer upon layer, making it impossible to climb over them. So, I would dive to go under the lowest grouping.

That worked, but then layers of lower wires appeared, taking me to the ground. So, I looked for holes in the web-like barrier. I would slip through a couple of holes, but then more wires would appear, closing those holes—that's when I'd wake up, shouting and grabbing at covers and pillows.

Years earlier I had read a book, *The Ravens*, by Christopher Robbins, which tells the story of USAF FAC (Forward Air Controller) pilots in Laos. I dug it up and leafed through it until I found the passage I needed—the author described the *exact and same nightmare*.

Wanting to understand, I tried to contact the author through the publisher but was unsuccessful. To this day, I have no explanation for the dream.

** PTSD **

"Nightmares"

"Frequent nightmares are a common symptom of PTSD. These nightmares may focus on the event that created the trauma or they may appear unrelated. Nightmares are different from flashbacks in that they occur on a subconscious level during sleep, while flashbacks take place while the mind is alert and awake."

—Angela, at facty.com, "10 Symptoms of PTSD," 21 May 2019

Hate war, love the American soldier.

—Lieutenant General Hal Moore

All gave some ... some gave all.

—Epithet for Veterans

Memorial Day, 1991: The Salute

After the success of the 1991 Gulf War, the consciousness of the American people had been piqued and patriotism was embraced. People unfurled flags, proudly displaying them in neighborhoods and commercial areas, enlistments were up, and Americans were proud of themselves and their armed forces.

Everyone was welcoming veterans home regularly, many times with television coverage on the six-o'clock news. The military had returned to its rightful place of prominence and respect, something that had vanished during the 1960s and 1970s.

I still didn't understand why America treated the military men and women of the Vietnam era so unfairly and with such disdain. That should not have happened. Even though Vietnam was our country's most unpopular war for some, Americans should not have taken leave of their senses, allowing stupidity and ignorance to flourish— yes, stupidity and ignorance.

Just remember how some people hailed the clowns that ran away to Canada or burned their draft cards as heroes, while characterizing the soldiers that went to Southeast Asia and did their duty as losers. And a few years later, Jimmy Carter rubbed salt into the collective wound of Vietnam vets when he pardoned those who fled to Canada—more stupidity and ignorance.

So, to reclaim some measure of dignity, I began a simple and very private ceremony. On Memorial Day and Veterans Day I would wear my ribbons and grab my Cav hat. I would leave for work a few minutes early and go downtown. On Federal Plaza, I would park my car and walk to the Vietnam War Memorial.

There I stood in front of the reflective stone and studied the etched names of Mahoning County's KIAs. Those men once lived in my community, and now all that remains of lives cut short in the service of their country was a carved list of their names.

I'm sure no bastard that fled to Canada ever gave them a thought. I'm sure not one draft-card burning son of a bitch could ever hold a candle to the courage of these dead soldiers. That these soldiers sacrificed themselves during such an ignorant era of American history makes their sacrifices more noble and more meaningful.

The memorial contains two names that I knew. Bruce Manton was the son of my sixth-grade teacher at Harding Elementary School. I recall him visiting his mom's classroom once, but regrettably I know nothing of his service and death. The other name is Edmond Saccomen. His nickname in high school was Slick. For four years, Ed sat in front of me in homeroom during high school. I don't know how he died either.

After a silent prayer, I would snap to attention and salute, holding it a few seconds, then I lowered my arm slowly. Returning to my car, I got on with the day's teaching.

I've been lucky so far—no one has interfered or distracted me during this private ritual. The closest folks have come to me are those driving by through the square. It's a good way to start two special days—putting things into perspective, keeping memories alive—and a reason to be thankful that I made it back alive.

Caution: Cape does not enable user to fly.

—Batman Halloween costume label, 1993

Summer 1991: Living Vicariously

Vietnam vets were never officially welcomed home as a group, even on Veterans Day in Washington when the Wall was dedicated. That event was the culmination of endeavors spearheaded and fulfilled by Vietnam veterans. The only thing the government did was to set aside land on the mall for the memorial—and that involved a long and drawn-out fight. So, coming home became an individual thing, without ceremony, without units marching in parades, without welcomes. But things would change.

***

My family welcomed me home first, ten years later, the city and county welcomed Vietnam vets with the dedication of the Vietnam Veterans Memorial Bridge in spring of 1983. I don't know if the state of Ohio formally welcomed us home. So, when Stormin' Norman Schwarzkopf marched down Pennsylvania Avenue in Washington DC after the Gulf War, I became emotional—as I lived that moment vicariously.

The country had experienced a resurgence in patriotism and had demonstrated support for the troops. Here was an event reminiscent of World War II victory celebrations. Now, consider the Vietnam War—think about what so many Americans were doing while we fought that war, and how they acted when we returned? It still hurts—will always hurt.

Allied forces that fought in Indochina were from Australia, New Zealand, the Philippines, the Republic of China, South Korea, Spain, South Vietnam and the USA.

Communist nations worldwide; China, Czechoslovakia, Cuba, East Germany, and the USSR supported the NVA and VC in Indochina.

We were not strong enough to drive out a half million American troops, but that wasn't our aim. Our intention was to break the will of the American government to continue the war. Westmoreland was wrong to expect that his superior firepower would grind us down. If we had focused on the balance of forces, we would have been defeated in two hours. We were waging a people's war ... America's sophisticated arms, electronic devices and all the rest were to no avail in the end. In war there are the two factors — human beings and weapons. Ultimately though, human beings are the decisive factor.

—General Vo Nguyen Giap,1990

February 1992: The Rest of the Story

A picture of Hueys is part of this memoir's entry, "2 May 1970: Day Two of the Cambodian Incursion." The caption describes an eight-slick Yellow Flight landing to refuel at Song Be. What follows is the rest of the story about that photo.

***

During April and May, a Cav photographer flew on many Masher birds, taxiing to Fire Support Bases and LZs throughout the Cav's AO. I'll call the photographer Specialist Sam Lensman. His pictures were of the highest quality, even artistic, and appeared in

1st Cav and other Army publications. I carried or encountered Sam many times, and he was eager to share his work with me and gave me dozens of glossy, black-and-white, 8x10s. I shared the photos with the members of our aircrews and kept some for myself.

One day, while flying Yellow 4 of a flight of eight, I noticed Sam taking pictures of our flight as we landed at Song Be to refuel. He was standing in the middle of the refueling area, photographing the Masher slicks. He couldn't be missed, and I made a mental note of it, remembering exactly where I was as Sam snapped away.

About a week later, I encountered Sam again and as usual; he showed me his latest batch of pictures. This time, he was unusually excited. Among the new shots were several of the Yellow Flight landing to the west ... at Song Be to refuel ... with me sitting in the Charlie Pop's seat of the Yellow 4 slick.

The pictures of the flight were amazingly clear and bordered on surreal. Sam caught the flight as it was changing formations, from sections-right to trail, to accommodate landing, to refuel. The Hueys appear to stack up and mesh as Sam captured them through his lens.

I was so glad I noticed Sam shooting away as we landed and then etched a mental note about it. Again, Sam gave me several copies of the fantastic Yellow flight sequence, which I shared with other Mashers.

As the weeks went by, I accumulated three or four dozen photos taken by Specialist Sam Lensman. Eventually Sam DEROSed and I never saw him again.

***

I first saw the book, *Incursion* by J.D. Coleman, in early 1992. The cover demanded that I buy and immediately devour the book. Its content, concerning the Cambodian invasion of May and June 1970, would spellbind since they discussed the events of flying into Cambodia with the Good Deal Company. The book's cover photo was the same picture Sam Lensman had given me back in May 1970.

Theresa Sepesy, 17 February 1928 to 7 September 1993.
(Author's private collection).

7 September 1993: Mom Died Today—PTSD, Part 8

After a long battle with liver cancer, my beautiful and loving mother died today.

When I arrived at the hospital, I sat on Mom's bed, as close to her as possible. Mom was in and out of consciousness, but we communicated—me speaking and Mom blinking her eyes or squeezing my hand in response. I remember her hazel eyes, looking at me, searching my face—and a tear formed. She was so weak but still fought for every breath. I told her I loved her.

As the hours passed, Mom slipped away more and more. We told her it was okay to let go, to go to God and her rest, and at 11:30 that evening on 7 September, Mom died. I was with her in the hospital room when she breathed her last.

***

I didn't cry at Mom's funeral, and I didn't know why for the longest time. To this day, I regret not having talked to Mom more about my years in the Army. I wanted to know how she got through that time, especially because I volunteered to go to Vietnam three times.

I recall one all-too-brief conversation during which I apologized to her for all the worry and pain I had caused. She told me she prayed nightly, and that she knew I would return safely. And she told me she knew flying in Vietnam was something I wanted to do.

I believed Mom because she was as strong as she was loving. But I ended that conversation without further questions because I didn't want to cause more pain for her.

I love you, Mom, and I miss you so very much. I wish I could hug you again. I love you.

***

According to Mom's death certificate, she died on 8 September. However, she died at 11:30PM on 7 September.

** PTSD **

"Emotional Numbing"

"It's very common for those with PTSD to try to numb their feelings. After all, it's hard to suffer pain when you don't feel any emotion at all. Emotional numbing often leads to the gradual withdrawal and eventually complete isolation from social circles. In time, the individual may find themselves socially isolated."

—Victor Camille Lebouthillier, "The Most Brutal Truth about PTSD," aliveforwellness.com

Do not fear the enemy, for they can take only your life. Fear the media far more, for they will destroy your honor.

—General Vo Nguyen Giap

1994: Cronkite Was Wrong, Schwarzkopf Was Right!

The Tet Offensive of January and February 1968 was over, and the VC and NVA were licking their wounds from a major ass-kicking. However, the media choose to follow another path of coverage, that of outrage and protest on the home front which played right into the hands of the NVA political strategy of waging war.

The fact is that the VC and elements of NVA reinforcements were decimated and operationally, set back one to two years—time needed to rearm and recuperate from that trouncing. That's a widely agreed to as fact, and references appear in many books about the war by both US and NVA military commanders. However, on 27 February 1968, CBS anchorman Walter Cronkite reported to America on his impressions of post-Tet Vietnam.

Cronkite set the tone by referring to his editorial as speculative, personal, and subjective, beginning with: "Who won and who lost in the great Tet offensive against the cities? I'm not sure. The Vietcong did not win by a knockout, but neither did we."

With his opening sentences, Cronkite presents a misinterpretation of an obvious enemy defeat. He continued by opining that another standoff might occur: "…Khe Sanh could well fall, with a terrible loss in American lives, prestige and morale…"

Cronkite was wrong about the fall of Khe Sanh.

The reporter continues with comments, both pro and con about the North Vietnamese and the US leadership, the possibilities of escalating military assets, invading the North, and the fear of using nuclear weapons which could lead to "cosmic disaster."

In closing, Cronkite skillfully couches his editorial with speculations about negotiation ploys, then opting for a middle-of-the-road assessment: "... we are mired in a stalemate."

But history shows, while well-intentioned, Cronkite was duped, just like so many other reporters who didn't understand the war and the complex levels of North Vietnamese strategies. In a time of social strife, Cronkite, sometimes referred to as America's most trusted man, did the country a disservice and helped turn citizens against their own military, weakened its diplomatic position, and strengthened the enemy's resolve.

Years later, I heard General Norman Schwarzkopf comment on Vietnam, where he served as a young Army officer. He put it this way: "Vietnam was overwhelmingly a victory for the American military. It was however, a political defeat."

That's exactly how it was—Schwarzkopf understood the enemy and the war much better than Cronkite.

Schwarzkopf's comment was vindication for me and thousands of other Vietnam veterans—I knew what I was talking about! I had been searching for a way to express myself for years, and now this eloquent warrior put it so succinctly and precisely. Thank you, Stormin' Norman, for setting the record straight.

Perhaps Cronkite and others in the media could have better served this country by exposing the political blundering and profiteering that hampered the military instead of spreading and fostering dissension throughout the nation that eventually manifested itself in the bad-mouthing of the military, alienating and discrediting the veterans, and then ignoring them.

The American fighting man in Vietnam fought, bled, and died just as bravely as any other soldier from any other war. The US never lost a major battle. More than 58,000 men and women gave their lives while fighting a tenacious and skilled enemy.

As Mashers of Bravo 227, we flew into the teeth of the enemy's defenses again and again, which eventually became a matter of routine. We were vulnerable to enemy fire from the moments of take-off to landing and then some. We fought while politicians at all levels of government ran for cover and chose the more attractive positions, usually anti-war, hoping for re-election. So, don't give me any more righteous crap about us losing the war!

In 1945, another internationally known reporter offered his observation about war, soldiers and journalists. Perhaps Walter would have reconsidered his comments if he had consulted with his colleague at CBS. Perhaps he could have applied Eric Sevareid's view to the larger picture of the war-scape that had developed in Vietnam. Consider the following comment from Sevareid.

> *Only the soldier really lives the war—the journalist does not. He may share the soldier's outward life and dangers, but he cannot share his inner life, because the same moral compulsion does not bear upon him.*
>
> *The observer knows he has alternatives of action—the soldier knows he has none. War happens inside a man and that is why, in a certain sense, you and your sons from the war will be forever strangers.*
>
> *If, by the miracle of art and genius in later years, two or three among them can open their hearts and the right words come, then perhaps, we shall know a little of what it was like, and we shall know then, that all the present speakers and writers hardly touch the story.*
>
> —CBS War Correspondent Eric Sevareid, Spring 1945

Thank you, Mr. Sevareid.

Question: What is the difference between a fairy tale and a war story?

Answer: A fairy tale begins with, "Once upon a time …" and a war story begins with, "There I was…." or "This is no shit!"

Autumn 1994: An Incredible Chance Meeting

This is no shit!

I recently gave my old flight jacket to my daughter, Jackie. She wore it from time to time, which led to an amazing crossing of paths.

***

I walked Jackie from the car to the ATA (American Taekwondo Association) school. She was wearing my flight jacket, complete with my unit patches. A couple of minutes later, a parent of another karate student approached me. "Is that your daughter?" asked the forty-ish father.

"Yes," I replied.

"Were you in the Cav?" he then asked, correctly deducing that the jacket originally belonged to me.

"Yes, I was. Were you?"

"Yeah, infantry."

"You guys had it rough. Which battalion were you with?"

"2nd of the 5th."

"I supported the 2nd of the 5th a few times. When were you there?"

"'70 and '71."

"Me too."

"Which unit were you in?" asked the veteran.

"Bravo 227," I said.

"Were you a gunner?"

"No, I was a pilot, Chief Warrant Officer."

"You guys were out of your minds," said the former grunt. "You'd fly anywhere. I'd never want to do that."

I'm sure both of us were thinking parallel thoughts: both in the Cav, in the same AO, at the same time—this conversation could become very interesting.

We introduced ourselves—the Skytrooper's name was Lenny.

"Tell me, Lenny, were you ever at Fire Support Base Ready?"

"Sure was."

"Were you there the night it got hit, a few hours after your insertion?"

"Yeah," he said with a bit of disbelief registering in his voice. "Don't tell me you flew us in."

"I'll be damned. Not only did my company combat assault you guys, I flew one of the birds that resupplied you that night during the attack."

Lenny and I then shared our impressions and memories of that day and night on 14 May 1970. I told Lenny how we were told not to shoot the tree line as we approached the beleaguered troops and about being in the left seat of the fourth bird and how grunts low-crawled to us to retrieve the ammo we brought for them. I told him about the grunt who stopped below me and looked up at me. Judging by his expression, he was scared half-to-death or amazed that we were sitting there, the perfect target for the NVA.

I wondered where Lenny was during the action so I asked him, "Were you one of those grunts who crawled to our Hueys to get the ammo?"

"No, another guy and I were stuck in the tree line with our M-60. We got separated from the guys in the LZ."

"Holy shit! We couldn't shoot up the tree line because your CO advised us that a machine gun team was somewhere out there. That was you!"

Both of us stood in amazement, shaking our heads, appreciating the moment and the unbelievable coincidences of the event. Lenny vividly recalled the terror of that night and how he and his gun-team member watched four Masher Hueys fly in with ammo during the NVA assault.

"We didn't dare move. When the NVA broke off their attack, we made our way back to the perimeter."

***

Once again, with matters of perspectives discussed, the question remains. Who's crazy?

Josy

1998: My Demon Dreams Continue—PTSD, Part 9

My reoccurring demon dreams are becoming more frequent, in groups and a couple times a week; then none or very few spread out over many weeks. Then the process repeats itself. It's been this way for years. But one night was extraordinary.

Once again, I dreamed I was being stalked by Viet Cong soldiers. The dream intensified as the shadowy figures with burning red eyes and wearing *non las* (conical hats) stood next to my bed. I sat upright and kicked the covers from my feet and swung my fists. The crashing of the tiffany lamp that was on the nightstand next to the bed and the pain in my hand awakened me.

Another demon dream that reoccurs is quite abstract. I'm in bed and cannot move. Amorphous-shaped pieces of metal slowly descend toward my chest and head. They appear to be large and heavy, some red and some metallic, with jagged and sharp edges and points—machines that are going to impale me.

The dreams end with me screaming, thrashing about, and kicking the covers. Sometimes I end up on my knees or standing on the mattress. When I know I'm fully awake, my heart is racing and I'm panting for breath. After I calm down, I'm afraid to fall back asleep.

** PTSD **

"Nightmares and PTSD"

"Nightmares are one of the 17 symptoms of PTSD. For example, a study comparing Vietnam Veterans to civilians showed that 52% of combat Veterans with PTSD had nightmares fairly often. Only 3% of the civilians in the study reported the same level of nightmares.

Other research has found even higher rates of nightmares. Of those with PTSD, 71% to 96% may have nightmares..."

—"Nightmares and PTSD: How Common Are Nightmares after Trauma?" from the US Department of Veterans Affairs; National Center for PTSD, 17 October 2019

On 20 March 1976, the government of Thailand ordered the closing of all US military bases.

March 2000 and 22 August 2000: Masher Huey 048

An article appeared in the March/April 2000 issue of the VHPA (Vietnam Helicopter Pilots Association) newsletter. Its title was "Information Sought on Vietnam, Huey." The first sentence mentioned the aircraft's butt number—048. I immediately recalled a Bravo Good Deal slick with that number. In fact, I remembered it being a real dog and underpowered.

The article's second paragraph mentioned 048's unit—Bravo 227, my unit. Of course, I was hooked and read on to learn that the curator of Motts Military Museum, in Groveport, just south of Columbus, Ohio had just obtained a Huey, 048, and needed information about it.

I called the article's contact person who guided me to the museum's curator, Warren Motts. Warren was thrilled to talk to me and wanted me to visit as soon as possible. Unfortunately, family and work would not allow that for six months, not until August. But, during that time, Warren and I talked on the phone extensively and I sent war memorabilia to him for the display he was building with his new Huey.

I sent Warren my logbook, a map or two, and patches. He was most interested in the log book because of entries I had made, showing I had flown 048 on several certain days.

Finally, on 22 August 2000, I drove to Groveport to meet Warren. A contingency of folks; Warren and his wife, Daisy, and about eight of their friends surprised me with their reception.

Masher Huey 048, at Fire Support Base Snuffy, Bu Gia Map (Courtesy of CW2 Trent Munsey, Masher 3-8).

Warren took me on a whirlwind tour of the museum's displays. Warren's museum was first rate, with glass-enclosed displays holding artifacts from the French and Indian War to present day.

The energetic curator was a meticulous historian—no detail too small, and his work reflected his interest and passion for American history. I understood why Warren had called me so many times with his many questions about 048, Bravo 227, and my memorabilia. The descriptive cards that were placed next to each artifact verified that.

During our initial talk, Warren expressed how important it was for him to not only present artifacts but to focus on their owner's connection. He wanted to show visitors that everyday people with stories about military service, war, and survival, people that fought for you and this great country, had owned and used the items on display. Above all, he wanted to tell the stories about those people connected to the displays. It was immediately apparent that Warren had lived up to this self-imposed requirement, and his museum showed that.

We made our way to the rear of the museum and I noticed some nervousness had come over me. We walked outside under the hot August sun and angled away from the building. There, about fifty yards away, sat 048, a part of Bravo 227, a part of me and my past. Warren's friends had gathered next to her.

Warren sensed I was getting emotional and said, "I'll give you some private time," and he joined his friends.

With each step toward 048 I was connecting with her, but this time, from a place far from Vietnam—forty yards, far away from Phuoc Vinh—thirty yards, now far from Ferguson Flyaway which filled my mind. My pulse quickened—at twenty yards I could feel it—combat assaults, taking fire, taking hits, Cambodia, Randy and Gary, Jeff and Butch.

She looked smaller, 048, like a person's elementary school room that's visited decades later. This Huey looked smaller—she seemed fragile but still dressed for battle.

At ten yards, my throat tightened—I felt that happen and needed a drink to moisten my mouth. I hoped I wouldn't break down like I did at the Wall in Washington. I swallowed hard and hoped to ease through the last ten yards.

So, I stopped and began a preflight-like look, taking in her rotor head and blades, the fuselage and tail boom. Then, without thinking and as if I was being pulled to the aircraft, I closed those final few yards and touched her nose—048. She was no longer the dog of an aircraft I had recalled six months earlier—she was 048, one of the Hueys I had flown in Vietnam with the Bravo Good Deal

Warren had moved his friends away from 048 and me. I was choking up and trembling, but nothing near my experience at the Wall. I circled 048, touching her skin; the door handle I had long ago twisted to open, the windows of the cargo door, the tail boom and horizontal stabilizer I had run my hand over, the tail stinger I would jump onto to check the tail rotor—no way I could do that now.

I moved toward the compartments forward of the tail boom and popped open one of them—just to do it, and looked at an empty inside. I went back to the left side and pulled open the AC's door—and the smell hit me, engulfed me, and took me back over three decades to the OD (Olive Drab green) Army in Vietnam. They say your sense of smell remains longer than one's other senses, somehow filing away those scents for future recall—I now know that to be true.

Warren joined me and introduced me to his cadre of museum volunteers and friends. They were all veterans, including a few Vietnam vets. After we exchanged pleasantries, I looked at Warren, "Can I sit in the AC's seat?"

"Joe, you can do whatever you want. This is your helicopter," and he took out a bunch of keys, handed them to one of his buddies and asked him to unlock the other doors.

I pulled myself into the left seat, awkwardly for sure, and sat down. My feet went forward automatically to the pedals and my hands to the collective and cyclic controls. *I was flying again, controlling this beautiful flying machine again.* I had settled into another mind-set, one from decades earlier—*I was home.*

Warren scooched down to my right rear with video camera in hand. He broke the spell, nevertheless, what a wonderful feeling.

For the next twenty minutes, Warren peppered me with questions about the helicopter's operation, the instrument panels and controls. I had to stop and think only one or two times, but most of the information needed for accurate answers popped out quickly.

Most of the commo and nav components were missing. I distinctly recall the Christmas tree (emergency light array) was also missing. Warren was filled with questions, and the smallest details of my answers thrilled him. For example, the window's pressure knob which was used to tighten the Plexiglas window in place—I showed him how it worked and he was like a little kid taking it all in. "I've been wondering what that knob was for."

"Can I climb on top," I asked.

"Like I said," answered Warren, "anything you like."

I climbed out of the AC's seat and stepped down and walked to the right side of 048. There I grabbed a handhold and pulled myself upwards, and pushed my feet through the flap-covered steps. Stepping toward the bird's topside, I gripped the last handhold and straightened up on top of her. I held the forward rotor blade for stability and edged toward the rotor mast and head. There I grabbed the silver stabilizer bar, and recalled how a bullet had torn through that heavy, grey mount.

I moved to the front and stooped down, careful not to snag an antenna, and looked through the greenhouse, then just allowed myself to ... to remember.

After a few more minutes, I climbed down from atop 048. Warren and I posed for many pictures together, with his friends, and the Huey.

Forty years after flying her in Vietnam, author with Masher Huey 048, at Motts Military Museum, August 2000 (Author's private collection).

We went inside and Warren showed me how he planned to expand the museum. He also wanted to know if I could stay overnight—Arnold Schwarzenegger was visiting the museum tomorrow. Warren had obtained Schwarzenegger's tank from the Austrian Army, which was now on display behind the museum with other vehicles and weapons.

Due to time, I declined. We thanked one another for the powerful and memorable visit, said goodbye, and I drove home, knowing I would return to take in the displays again, but more deliberately and without the commotion and emotion of reuniting with 048.

"And who was wrong … and who was right? And did it matter in the thick of the fight?"

—Billy Joel, "Goodnight Saigon"

Veterans Day, 2001: On the Air

My brother, Eddie, and his wife, JoAnn, knew a disc jockey at the classic rock station, Y-103. Lynn Davis had read about 048 and me in a Vindicator article and asked Eddie to put me in contact with her. She wanted me to join her on her annual Veterans Day show.

After a couple of phone calls, Lynn and I met at the station. I stopped by and learned about what I could expect while on the air. Lynn was excited that I agreed to be on her show.

On Veterans Day I took half of a personal day and arrived at Y-103 precisely at 11:00AM, just when Lynn expected me. I looked through the large plate-glass window and caught her eye—she motioned me to come inside. A song was playing, so it was okay to talk. Lynn introduced me to Jim, who had served in the Gulf War in 1991 with the Pennsylvania National Guard unit that a SCUD missile had struck, killing thirteen and wounding fifty-six soldiers.

Lynn introduced me to Monty, a Vietnam vet who had served at Tuy Hoa in 1971, a place I knew well. During a rocket attack, an ammo dump exploded, injuring Monty. Because of his injuries, Monty couldn't work, however the VA had compensated him for his service-connected injury.

Lynn began her show by introducing her three guest veterans. She had each one of us tell when and where we served, our unit and military specialty. I was more nervous than I had expected and had dry mouth. But Lynn had pop and pizza for us, and that solved the dry-mouth problem and helping to loosen things up as the broadcast minutes ticked by.

While songs played, Lynn would chat with us or listen to us tell war stories among ourselves. When she heard something that she liked, she would tell that person to retell that story on the air. When my turns came around, I spoke about the invasion of Cambodia and how the war had become known as the rock 'n' roll war and the TV war.

Lynn loved the story about running combat assaults while "Spirit in the Sky" and "Magic Carpet Ride" played in the background on the NAV radio. I described it as living a surreal reality. That story fit perfectly because Y-103 is a classic rock radio station.

I also explained the daily routine of flying for a 1st Cav line-company and how the Bravo Good Dealers just did their jobs day after day.

All of us got into a conversation about Hollywood's portrayal of the Vietnam War. I said *Apocalypse Now* and *Deer Hunter* were both gross exaggerations of the war and conduct of US military personnel. Yes, even though *Deer Hunter* won the Oscar for best picture, it presented a ludicrous story about soldiers' tours of duty and survival in Vietnam.

Apocalypse Now was an absolute joke and degraded the American fighting man in Vietnam—I hated it. Even *Platoon*, another Oscar winner for best picture, focused on an unbelievable rivalry between sergeants and the men in their unit.

Lynn kept feeding me questions and gave me more air-time between requests called in by listeners. The lines were so busy that my sister, Kathy, couldn't get through to make a request until well after the show. So, Lynn kept track of those requested tunes and played them on the following day.

I described how demanding the flying of May and June 1970 had been with the Cambodian invasion, but what a tremendous training ground it was for a new-guy pilot like me. I also shared pictures with Lynn, Monty, and Jim.

Since we were on a classic rock station, we of course talked about the music of the Vietnam era, in particular the groups and tunes that we liked the most. I mentioned Santana, Creedence Clearwater Revival and the Moody Blues, and talked about how every show in the officers' club ended with the band playing the Animals' "We Gotta Get out of This Place."

Lynn chatted with other vets on the air and played each of the five services' songs. Someone requested another Animals' tune, "Sky Pilot," which Lynn gladly played. After the song ended, I asked who knew what a sky pilot was. No one knew that a sky pilot was the nickname for a chaplain. So, that was everyone's trivia lesson for the day.

Our three hours of on-the-air time flew by. Lynn wanted to end the show at 2:00 but it was going so well with requests and discussion we stayed on the air until a little before 3:00 when the next DJ came in. Lynn thanked us and invited us back for the next year's show. She had been paying attention to the earlier conversations and ended the show by playing "We Gotta Get out of This Place."

Being on the radio had been quite an experience, and it tired me. But I was already looking forward to next year's show.

Y-103, disc jockey Lynn Davis, every veteran's best friend, with the author on Veterans Day 2001 (Author's private collection).

Political and self-serving interests prompted membership in SEATO in September 1954, as did withdrawals by Pakistan and France, beginning in the early 1970s. Thereafter, and with the end of the Vietnam War, SEATO was dissolved on 30 June 1977.

26 December 2001: The Greatest Generation Gathers at the Kitchen Table

I had been meaning to do this for years. So, after all the well-deserved recognition of World War II veterans and the dedication of the World War II Memorial in Washington DC, I decided it was time. I invited Dad, Uncle Frank, and Uncle Al to the house to document their experiences during their war.

We gathered around the kitchen table and the trio of elderly Sepesys took turns responding to dozens of questions I had prepared. As a result, I finally got a timeline straight in my head about Dad's service in the Marine Corps, Uncle Frank on the USS *Ben Franklin*, and Uncle Al's service in China. I found it interesting that all three went west to the Pacific and Asian theaters of operation.

At the end of the discussion, I told them how I would write an account of each brother's service and give copies of all three accounts to everyone in the family; brothers, sisters, and cousins.

Uncle Al asked, "Where's your story?"

I answered in a semi-serious tone, "That could be a book."

"Well, get started."

At that moment I decided to write my memoir for the same reason I documented the stories of Dad, and Uncles Frank and Al—for the family to know, understand, and remember. I did not know how long the memoir would be, how I would approach the task, or how it would take shape—but I would do it.

A week later, my sister, Monica, did the same thing as me, except she one-upped me by video-taping the three brothers and WWII vets. Well done, Monica.

About a month later, I completed all three accounts and distributed them to the family. Later, Monica enhanced my written accounts with pictures of each Sepesy during his years of service. The pictures were a nice touch and added to the documentation immensely.

Gathering with my Dad and two uncles was one of the most satisfying and meaningful encounters I had ever experienced. I'm very glad I wrote their accounts and my only regret was waiting so long to do so.

1978 through 1984: The Democratic Republic of Vietnam battled Cambodians, Chinese, and Thais in a series of incursions along mutual borders.

Summer 2002: Jackie and I Visit Motts Military Museum

My daughter, Jackie, and I visited Motts Military Museum today. Warren escorted us to 048 and unlocked her so we could take pictures and explore the aircraft. Jackie was excited, which made me feel very good. That she was interested in what I did in the Army was special.

The author with his daughter, Jacqueline Noelle, posing by Masher Huey 048 at Motts Military Museum, summer 2002. (Author's private collection).

I don't mean to badmouth youth, but it's been my experience that many kids, especially girls, don't know or care to know about any aspect of the military, including the experiences of relatives.

I donated my log book, helmet, uniform and other memorabilia to Warren. Receiving the flight helmet, as banged up as it was, pleased him very much.

Warren told us he was expanding the museum by building a wing for the Vietnam era and the USA's military operations beyond that. One display would feature my memorabilia because of my connection with 048.

***

Five years later, Warren would tell me something I had not known about this visit, something that moved him emotionally, something he would never forget. That something did not involve me directly—it involved my daughter, Jackie.

Veterans Day, 2002: On the Air Again at Y-103

Lynn Davis invited me to her annual Veterans show on Y-103. This time, Monty and I were the only guests. Lynn had me repeat the Rock 'n' Roll war story involving running CAs with "Spirit in the Sky" and "Magic Carpet Ride" playing on the NAV radio in the background—my surrealistic reality story. Lynn said it was one of the highlights of last year's show, which made me feel good about my participation in this year's event.

As I neared the end of the story, Lynn started playing "Spirit in the Sky" in the background, then increased the volume as I ended my narration. For me that was reminiscent of the mission and it took me back to Nam, flying Hueys with the Bravo Good Deal. Lynn had a way, a style about her presentation. She was a pro!

When Lynn asked for more stories, I spoke about the emergency night resupply at LZ Ready and the subsequent chance meeting with Lenny at Jackie's karate school. When Lynn asked for a lighter story, I spoke about flying in my underwear during a rocket attack. Of course, she led me to tell that story during the next talk segment.

Lynn always tried to get messages across to her listening audience, messages about patriotism and the human angle—much like Warren Motts and his philosophy concerning the presentation and display of artifacts at his museum.

Toward the end of the show and with that in mind I spoke about documenting the wartime experiences of Dad, Uncle Frank and Uncle Al, explaining what a gratifying experience it was. Of course, Lynn picked up on that and messaged her audience, "That *greatest generation*, now in their eighties and nineties, is quickly passing away. Now is the time for all of us to approach our relatives and friends and document their experiences."

To emphasize her comment, she then played each of the five services' songs. Then, after thanking Monty and myself, she again ended the show with "We Gotta Get out of This Place" by the Animals.

"Leadership is a highly personal, individual matter. Each leader must establish his own approach based on an internal compass using a method geared to his personality, his capabilities but always oriented towards accomplishing the mission while knowing and taking care of his men."

—Harold G. Moore, *Hal Moore on Leadership: Winning When Outgunned and Outmanned,* Magnum Books, 2019

7 January 1979: Vietnamese forces overthrew the Pol Pot regime in Cambodia.

9 January 2003: Bobby Cowen Died Today

Bobby Cowen died today, but I didn't know about his final departure until I read the obituaries in the July/August issue of the newsletter of the Vietnam Helicopter Pilots Association.

I wish I had thought about him before I got into this memoir. I would have written or called him just to thank him for having faith in me when I was a WOC trying to fly an OH-23 at Fort Wolters. That was one of those *shoulda—woulda—coulda* moments we all experience during a lifetime.

Mr. Cowen's obituary gave me information that I had never known about him. He was a California boy from Monterey, was in the top ten of his flight school class, WORWAC 65-1 at Fort Rucker; and he was awarded the Purple Heart.

After separating from the Army, Mr. Cowen became a civilian flight instructor for the US Army at Fort Wolters, Texas, where I met him in June 1969. When the Army cut back on the number of flight instructors, Mr. Cowen flew civilian helicopters in northern California and Quebec, Canada. Later in life, the VA diagnosed him with PTSD and diabetes, which ultimately caused his death.

So, here's to you, Bobby Cowen, CW2 Robert Howard Cowen, 10 April 1945 to 9 January 2003, one hell of a pilot, one damn fine IP, and my friend. I wonder what he saw in me. Thank you, Mr. Cowen, God bless you, and rest in a well-deserved peace.

Send in the First Team, destroy the Republican Guard.
Let's go home.

—*"Stormin'"* Norman Schwarzkopf, speaks of his respect
for the 1st Cavalry Division during Operations
Desert Shield and Desert Storm, 1991

"They Served"
...reliving memories
that will not die
giving their all
for you and I -
friends taken
lives shaken..."

—Muse, *Enigmatic Evolution*, Create Space, 2010

17 March 2003: Operation Iraqi Freedom

I woke up wanting to feel relieved because the war was finally underway—like waiting for a mission to begin and finally taking off and flying to the LZ. But inexplicably, things didn't sit right with me—I was uncomfortable. No, that modifier fell short—my uneasiness was more intense, and I was nervous. But that, too, did not describe the acute tightness that manifested itself throughout my body. I was hyper-vigilant—just like flying in Vietnam. Much to my dismay, I determined it was fear that held me.

I equated it to the feeling I experienced in the bunker during my first mortar attack, and then all those missions I flew I knew would be dangerous, already discussed in this memoir. But why, why such feelings today? I was a spectator, safe and far away from the event. Then it came to me, the parallel I could not have drawn before this time, involving another approaching war.

Dad cried when I left for Nam because he knew. That's why I had been near tears. I was feeling like Dad felt for me when I left for war, now feeling the same way for all of our soldiers marching into battle. I felt fear for them because I now knew, yes, *I now knew*.

Being a father, the concept of family had a greater meaning. This revelation was nothing new for humanity, but it was my turn to experience it. The right set of factors was in place, and I had lived the right set of experiences.

While driving to work, I cried, releasing some pent-up emotion that had been gathering throughout the military build-up and the daily news reports of impending war—and that was good. I didn't realize that, but it was good.

24 November 1979, the US General Accounting Office verified that thousands of US troops had been exposed to the herbicide known as Agent Orange while in Vietnam.

Veterans Day, 13 November 1982: The Vietnam War Memorial was dedicated in Washington DC. Over 58,000 names of servicemen and women killed during the war, are inscribed on its wall.

28 January 1983: President Ronald Reagan said that a full accounting of American POWs and MIAs in southeast Asia is a "…. highest national priority…."

5 July 1983: In federal court, released documents proved that the Dow Chemical Company knew in the mid-1960s, that exposure to dioxins in Agent Orange might cause serious illness and death—but the company withheld that information so the herbicides could be sold to the US Army.

7 May 1984: A class-action suit brought by 150,000 Vietnam veterans against seven chemical companies settle out of court for $180,000,000.

31 March 2003: An Announcement

The year 2003 would be an interesting year regarding my military experiences over three decades earlier. Induction to the Ohio Military Hall of Fame for Valor would be the highlight.

On 31 March, an article in the *Vindicator* announced that honor. I received many phone calls and cards of congratulations. Of course, members of my family responded, but other contacts were unexpected. I received congratulations from school and YEA personnel, former employers and teachers, and friends.

This honor would not come without a price. It would signal the intensification of my PTSD in the most profound ways and eventually lead to the much-needed help of psychological professionals at the VA. But, for the moment, this personal recognition felt great.

2 May 2003: US Army nurse, 1ˢᵗ Lieutenant Sharon Lane, was inducted into the Ohio Military Hall of Fame for Valor. She was the first and only American nurse to be killed in action in South Vietnam, the result of an enemy barrage.

2 May 2003: Induction, Ohio Military Hall of Fame for Valor

The Components of the
Ohio Military Hall of Fame Medal

The green wreath is in memory of the soldiers who died in battle, but are not forgotten.

The cross is not a religious symbol, but represents the four corners of the world in which the US military has served.

The eagle represents service in a national military branch of service.

The outline and flag of Ohio indicate that the medal's recipient was born in the State of Ohio or was inducted into a national branch of service while in the State of Ohio.

To avoid confusion with other awards, and so there is no doubt for why the medal was awarded, the word "VALOR" is displayed prominently.

The red and white ribbon attached to the medal is symbolic of the blood that was shed and the lives that were lost.

The colors, red, white, and blue, symbolize the flags of the United States and Ohio.

Members of my family gathered on Soldiers Plaza on the east side of the Capitol's grounds. In attendance were Jackie, my daughter; my siblings, Steve, Eddie and his wife JoAnn, Monica and her husband Richie along with sons, Sage and Hayden, and Dad in his Marine Corps League red blazer. Uncle Frank cut short his USS *Ben Franklin* reunion to attend. He wore a windbreaker that said, "USS *Ben Franklin*, the Ship that Wouldn't Die." My cousin Davy drove Uncle Al and Aunt Theresa to the event.

The fourth group, the Class of '03, comprised twelve Ohioans, was about to be inducted into the Ohio Military Hall of Fame for Valor.

The medal presented by the Ohio Military Hall of Fame for Valor (Author's private collection).

Warren Motts greeted us as we arrived and introduced me to the other inductees and a few members of the OMHFV from the three previous classes. He introduced me to Ron Rosser, Medal of Honor recipient from the Korean War. I was in awe and tongue-tied, wanting to talk to him but at a loss for words. Even more awesome was Ron congratulating me on my special day. Imagine, a Medal of Honor recipient congratulating me on my induction to the OMHFV. Ron received the Hall's number-one medal in May 2000, the first class of inductees.

I mingled for a while, greeting family members as they arrived, and thanked them for attending to watch a family member honored in such a fine way. My sister,

Monica, served as the unofficial photographer and took some beautiful pictures of the ceremony and family group.

I was to be the last inductee on this day so I took my place in the front row, seat number twelve. A Green Beret Technical Sergeant sat next to me. We chatted a bit, and I learned he served in Vietnam at the same time as me during my first tour. He

The author receives the Ohio Military Hall of Fame for Valor medal from US Congressman Patrick J. Tiberi. The inscription on the back of the medal has my name and, "Number 48, Class of 2003." I was the forty-eighth member of the Hall and a member of the class of 2003. (Author's private collection).

was in II Corps, operating out of Nha Trang. He told me about being extracted from the jungle at the end of a mission—the Huey dragged him through treetops while he dangled from a rope, eighty feet below.

Also, present was the mother of US Army nurse, 1st Lieutenant Sharon Lane, who was killed during a rocket attack on the 312th Evacuation Hospital in Vietnam. Instead of taking cover, Lt. Lane rushed to move patients in her ward to safety. A 122mm rocket exploded, killing her. Lieutenant Lane's selfless courage exemplifies the willingness of military personnel to perform their duties, despite endangering their own lives—that band-of-brothers mentality.

On 12 April 1983, after much study concerning a separate branch, the Department of the Army announced the birth of its new, Aviation Branch. (Courtesy of the US Army).

Summer 2003: Aftermath

After my induction into the OMHFV, I received cards and phone calls from well-wishers, some I had not seen or heard from in years.

The *Boardman Town Crier* also ran a story of the induction in its 8 May 2003 edition. I received congratulations from people four months after the news articles: from a new doctor during an appointment, a complete stranger while working at the university, and a clerk in a department store.

During the summer I spoke before three groups. Monica's cub-scout troop invited me to talk to the boys and their parents. The boys had many questions and asked about helicopters, the missions, and the medals and pictures I had brought. It was special because my nephews, Sage and Hayden, were there and presented me with a notebook of artwork and writings. And Monica taught them well—every boy said, "Welcome home," or, "Thank you for your service." I got choked up.

I also spoke to the United Veterans Council in their log cabin on the Canfield Fair Grounds, and the Marine Corps League at their monthly meeting. I told about the ridgeline mission where the .51 cal rounds passed through my bird, touching no one or nothing—the same story in which the ARVN unit refused to move from the ridge, so we had to extract them a few hours later. I also spoke about the friendly fire mission in which my flight was told not to return fire, even if fired upon. I explained how the province chiefs had to approve missions three days ahead of time, wanting these WWII vets to know just how crazy things were.

I then asked for questions—there were none, not one damned question.

That troubled me. That sentiment from the sixties and seventies was still clear in segments of society. Again, veterans displayed a disinterest, similar to my experience at the PLAV with Dad, upon returning from Vietnam. I believed I was wasting my time. I turned down all subsequent invitations to such meetings.

While speaking at the United Veterans Council meeting, I met John Twohig again. Of course, we remembered each other from the 107th in 1973 and 1974. After saying hello John expressed his shock at my appearance—how crooked my posture was.

I had already decided on back operation number three for early 2004. My vertebrae had slipped three quarters of an inch above the fused vertebrae, and that condition had to be eased. Two conservative surgeons did not hesitate in advising me that another operation was in order as soon as they viewed the x-rays. They feared that a sudden jolt would sever the spinal cord near the point of fusion.

John asked if I had filed a claim with the VA. I explained I had done so in 1974 and that the VA denied my claim. John said it was time to re-file.

I was reluctant because I knew that no military medical records about my back existed. But John explained the laws had changed and was confident I would win. So, with his help, we refiled my claim with the VA through the AMVETS to begin the drawn-out process all over again.

Dad introduced me to Bob Brienik, the director of volunteers at the Youngstown VA clinic. He was interested in helping me get my correct medals and set my record of military duty straight. About eighteen months later, we were partially successful. There still was no accounting for two DFCs (Distinguished Flying Crosses). Also, orders for a Purple Heart were denied, and documentation about the third Air Medal for Valor could not be located—frustrating.

"Magic Carpet Ride"
"I like to dream yes, yes, right between my sound
machine
On a cloud of sound I drift in the night
Any place it goes is right
Goes far, flies near, to the stars away from here
Well, you don't know what we can find
Why don't you come with me little girl
On a magic carpet ride…."

—Steppenwolf, 1968

Veterans Day, 2003: Third Time on the Airwaves at Y-103

Two Airmen from the Vienna airbase, Tom and Dan, joined Jim, Monty, and me on the air with Lynn Davis. Tom and Dan were members of the 910th Tactical Airlift Squadron and had served in Iraq. A young Marine lieutenant named Josh was also there. He had just returned from Fallujah, in Iraq, and its hellacious fighting, and was home on leave.

I wore my Cav hat and blazer with medals. Lynn asked me to discuss the medals, so I briefly described two of them. She also asked me to talk about my induction into the Ohio Military Hall of Fame for Valor. I focused on the camaraderie and emotion, my family in attendance, and meeting Medal of Honor recipient Ron Rosser.

Relevant to Vietnam, I talked about the invasion of Cambodia and the combat assault during which I carried a CBS cameraman. My last account was about the friendly fire combat assault near Bong Son, for which we were told to not return fire because it would be friendly.

The show went on without a hitch, and after signing off, Lynn invited me back for the next year. Then I spoke briefly with Josh. I wished him good luck since he was returning to combat in Iraq. I told him, "Josh, remember three words—don't become complacent." Josh understood.

Veterans Day, 11 November 1984: A statue depicting three soldiers was dedicated at the Vietnam War Memorial.

Veterans Day, 11 November 1993: A statue depicting nurses was dedicated at the Vietnam War Memorial.

February and March 2004: Back Operations 3 and 4

Another busy and interesting year began with back operation three on 6 February at the Cleveland Clinic.

Because John Twohig and I had reopened my VA claim, I wrote a lengthy letter to Randy Clark, Masher 2-2 and WORWAC 69-49 classmate. We hadn't talked since 1974, and I was hoping to re-establish our friendship. I also thought Randy could help me get in contact with other Bravo Good Dealers that knew about my shoot-down of 18 April 1970. I timed the mailing of the letter so Randy would receive it while I was recuperating.

A week after the operation, the phone rang. I recognized the voice immediately, even though thirty years had passed—it was Masher 2-2, Randy Clark. Unfortunately, I sounded horrible because of bruised vocal cords caused by intubation during my operation, which lasted ten-and-one-half hours. I wasn't supposed to talk, so I made the call short.

I told Randy that I'd call him when I felt better and my voice improved. In the meantime, Randy got to work within his network of Bravo Good Dealers that he had been communicating with for years on the internet and telephone—he was determined to help me.

I expressed my gratitude and told him I didn't want him to go to any trouble, fighting my battle for me—then he cut me off, "Hey," he said, "would you do the same thing for me?"

"Of course, I would."

"Then shut up. We were Mashers and we're still Mashers!"

That exchange was my first experience with the band-of-brothers connection, its mystique—whatever one wants to call it. The passage of time or circumstances did not matter—we were still Bravo Good Dealers, bound by the life and death events encountered day in and day out in Vietnam. I would learn just how intense that connection could be in the next couple of years.

About a week later, I called Randy, and we got caught up on each other's lives. He put me in contact with several Bravo Good Dealers, so I started writing letters and making telephone calls. Afterwards, I received only one report from a former door gunner, John Goosman, He knew all about my shoot-down and its unique circumstances. Not only did this soldier confirm the story, he also told me that there was a running joke with the enlisted men I had never realized. "Don't fly with Joey— he got shot down and didn't even know it."

On 26 March 2004, I returned to the Cleveland Clinic for corrective surgery—back operation number four. X-rays showed the newly placed metal implants had somehow opened and a dangerous situation existed that required immediate, corrective surgery.

I'm sure the doctor was afraid I was going to sue, but I gave him every indication that I just wanted the damn thing fixed once and for all. But another problem developed—the tops of my thighs were tingling or would go numb. Thankfully, this condition slowly dissipated over the next few years.

I underwent an eight-and-one-half hour operation. Because the locking mechanism had not been tightened, a loose three-inch screw rubbed and widened one hole that had been drilled through a vertebra. To secure that area of my back, the doctor fused L6 to L5 through L3 with screws and titanium implants. There was still no guarantee that I wouldn't need another operation. And something new, advancing nerve damage would begin to change my body.

From time to time, the tree of liberty must be watered with
the blood of tyrants and patriots.

—Thomas Jefferson

June 2004: I Cried—PTSD, Part 10

I saw the movie; *We Were Soldiers Once, and Young*, an account of the Battle of LZ X-Ray in November 1965. It was the first major battle of the war, in which elements of the 1st Cavalry Division met hardened NVA troops. The battle occurred near highway 14, near Plei Djereng, south of Pleiku in II Corps, an area I became familiar with during my second tour.

The movie depicted how Moore's battalion formed, trained and fought in Vietnam. I know I'm minimizing things, but the blood-and-guts parts are authentic and illustrate how the battle was a learning experience for both US and NVA combatants. The NVA learned that running into an LZ with an AK-47 was not conducive to living and victory, and the Cav learned its lesson about the tenacity and tactics of the enemy. In the end, casualties were high on both sides, but Lieutenant Colonel Hal Moore and the 1st of the 7th held their ground.

I was fine during the movie, until its end, after the battle scenes. I started choking up when LTC Moore and his unit returned home. Then I lost it. My throat tightened and tears flowed, so I stopped fighting it and just let the emotion out and cried at my seat.

After the credits rolled, I left the theater. I was not the only Vietnam vet who had seen the movie. Two other, middle-aged men with reddened eyes were also leaving the theater. We looked at each other and nodded. We knew we were Vietnam veterans.

***

For the past two years I had been encountering other problems, especially at work, becoming embroiled with confrontations involving the administration, students and parents, and colleagues—time to ponder.

"No recovery from trauma is possible without attending to issues of safety, care for the self, reparative connections to other human beings, and a renewed faith in the universe. The therapist's job is not just to be a witness to this process but to teach the patient how."

—Janina Fisher, *Healing the Fragmented Selves of Trauma Survival: Overcoming Internal Self-Alienation*, Rutledge, 2017

On St. Crispin's Day, 25 October 1415, King Henry V of England inspired his soldiers, referring to them as his "band of brothers." He urged his greatly outnumbered men to face the French force, telling them that years from now, they would be proud, recalling how they fought with Henry and were victorious in this, the Battle of Agincourt.

"King Henry V's St. Crispin's Day Speech"

"What's he that wishes so?
My cousin Westmoreland? No, my fair cousin;
If we are mark'd to die, we are enow
To do our country loss; and if to live,
The fewer men, the greater share of honor.
God's will! I pray thee, wish not one man more.
By Jove, I am not covetous for gold,
Nor care I who doth feed upon my cost;
It yearns me not if men my garments wear;
Such outward things dwell not in my desires.
But if it be a sin to covet honor,
I am the most offending soul alive.
No, faith, my coz, wish not a man from England.
God's peace! I would not lose so great an honor
As one man more methinks would share from me
For the best hope I have. O, do not wish one more!
Rather proclaim it, 'Westmoreland, through my host
That he which hath no stomach to this fight,
Let him depart; his passport shall be made,
And crowns for convoy put into his purse;
We would not die in that man's company
That fears his fellowship to die with us.
This day is call'd the feast of Crispian.
He that outlives this day, and comes safe home,
Will stand a tip-toe when this day is nam'd,
And rouse him at the name of Crispian.
He that shall live this day, and see old age,
Will yearly on the vigil feast his neighbors,
And say 'To-morrow is Saint Crispian.'

Then will he strip his sleeve and show his scars,
And say 'These wounds I had on Crispian's day.'
Old men forget; yet all shall be forgot,
But he'll remember, with advantages,
What feats he did that day. Then shall our names,
Familiar in his mouth as household words-
Harry the King, Bedford and Exeter,
Warwick and Talbot, Salisbury and Gloucester-
Be in their flowing cups freshly rememb'red.
This story shall the good man teach his son;
And Crispin Crispian shall ne'er go by,
From this day to the ending of the world,
But we in it shall be remembered-
We few, we happy few, we band of brothers;
For he to-day that sheds his blood with me
Shall be my brother; be he ne'er so vile,
This day shall gentle his condition;
And gentlemen in England now-a-bed
Shall think themselves accurs'd they were not here,
And hold their manhoods cheap whiles any speaks
That fought with us upon Saint Crispin's day."

—William Shakespeare, 1599

August 2004: The Best Reunion—Band of Brothers, Part 4

Randy called—he was on Route 224 heading east toward my home, just minutes away. "Four lights, turn right onto Parkside, bear left at the fork...."

Five minutes later, Randy parked his car in the driveway and got out. I recognized him immediately, despite thirty-plus years of separation. We hugged and laughed, took a good look at each other and hugged again. We went inside and after introductions settled in the family room.

120

It was so cool—I was looking at Masher 2-2 and he was looking at Masher 2-4. It didn't matter that such a long time had passed since we last saw each other. That was inconsequential, and it felt like yesterday when we were flying Hueys in Vietnam, watching out for each other and counting the days to DEROS.

Randy was flying big jets for USAir trans-Atlantic flights, usually to England and Germany. He was twice-divorced and had a beautiful thirteen-year-old daughter. He owned two homes, one in Greensboro, North Carolina, and the other near Philadelphia, Pennsylvania.

We talked about my four back operations and the recovery process. We went to a local restaurant where we talked and talked and talked. There was absolutely no

After 31 years, the author and Randy Clark reunite. (Author's private collection).

uneasiness and no shortage of words or topics for discussion. Again, it was so cool to be with a fellow Bravo Good Dealer.

When we got back home, Randy and I went through my photo albums and I updated him on the 048 story and being inducted into the OMHOFV. Then, he showed a ninety-minute video he had made from eight-millimeter footage he had shot in Vietnam— home movies of the war. Jackie got to see me as a nineteen-year-old, hot-shot pilot in Phuoc Vinh.

We enjoyed the film immensely and recalled people and stories. And this was very curious—Randy spotted me in a volley-ball scene and he noticed my back. I wasn't wearing a shirt, and he immediately commented about how crooked my back appeared and that I stood and moved in an odd sort of way.

After viewing pictures and Randy's video, how much we remembered, and didn't remember, and how one thought cued another to the forefront of one's mind amazed us. I remember taking a few rough notes for this memoir.

The next morning Randy and I had breakfast at Perkins, made our goodbyes and promised to stay in touch and visit regularly. I watched Randy pull away and make his way to Route 11. Before Randy left, I told him about my radio appearances on Y-103 and that he should tune in that station as he drove away from Canfield.

After Randy drove from sight, I called the station hoping to get through to Lynn Davis who was on the air. After a dozen rings, she answered. I asked her— actually pleaded with her to play "Spirit in the Sky" and make it a special request for Masher 2-2.

Lynn recalled my rock 'n' roll war story and the significance of the song. I explained why my request was so special today because of my reunion with Randy. She understood how important and extraordinary my request was and that she would fit the song in.

A minute later, the song that was playing on the radio ended and Lynn spoke, "Masher twenty-two," she said, not 2-2—but that was okay. "Masher twenty-two, this next song is for you from your good buddy Masher twenty-four."

The base line of "Spirit in the Sky" started playing in the background as Lynn continued. "Hope your drive is safe and you enjoy this special request. This is for you, Masher twenty-two, and thank you for your service."

Wow, I thought. I hoped Randy was listening, and he felt as good as I did after hearing Lynn take my request. She put the request on so quickly and made a perfect introduction. It truly was a special request and once again, Lynn proved she was every veterans' best friend.

When the song ended, Lynn said some nice things about me regarding her Veterans Day show and thanked all Vietnam vets for their service. As she started the next tune, my phone rang—it was Randy.

"I haven't heard my call-sign in ..." he choked up, "Do you know when the last time I heard my call-sign over the air was?"

The excitement in Randy's voice was apparent as well as the disbelief. "About thirty-three years," I answered. "How did you like the request I called in?"

"Joey, I didn't believe what I was hearing. It was a surreal moment. Then it sunk in and it got to me. I had to pull over because I started to cry."

"I'm going to tell Lynn just how special that request turned out to be," I said. "She has no idea how meaningful the moment was."

"Tell her I said thank you. Two-two, out."

"Roger that. Two-four, out."

I didn't tell Lynn the entire story until much later. She loved it and it touched her not only because of how special it was but because it involved vets. She realized how important such a gesture could be to a vet. Knowing how Randy heard his call-sign and got so emotional was the proof.

"It's something special," I explained, "that band-of-brother's thing."

***

Randy's movies contained many scenes of Phuoc Vinh and the Bravo Good Dealers flying in the AO. His movies also contained footage of our last flight, from Katum to Papa Vic. Refer to entry, "18 March 1971: Final Artillery Clearance," in *Volume I.*

Doug Bradley and Craig Werner have compiled a list of songs they consider as the top-ten during the Vietnam War. Numbers 10 to 2, here are:

10. "Green Green Grass of Home" by Porter Wagoner

9. "Chain of Fools" by Aretha Franklin

8. "The Letter" by the Box Tops

7. "(Sittin' on) The Dock of the Bay" by Otis Redding

6. "Fortunate Son" by Creedence Clearwater Revival

5. "Purple Haze" by Jimi Hendrix

4. "Detroit City" by Bobby Bare

3. "Leaving on a Jet Plane" by Peter, Paul and Mary

2. "I Feel Like I'm Fixin' to Die Rag" by Country Joe & The Fish

—Doug Bradley and Craig Werner, *We Gotta Get Out of This Place: The Soundtrack of the Vietnam War (Culture and Politics in the Cold War and Beyond),* University of Massachusetts Press, 21 October 2015

Veterans Day, 2004: Y-103, the Fourth Time

The broadcast booth for Lynn Davis's Veterans Day show was more crowded this year. Monty, Jim and I were there along with Dan and Tom from the 910th in Vienna. And Josh, the Marine lieutenant, had completed his tour in Iraq safely and returned to stateside.

I was the last to arrive and the only open seat was next to someone I didn't know, an imposing figure, huge and bald, with one front tooth missing. He was grossly overweight and had tattoos all over his exposed skin. I'll call him Scorpion.

After introductions, I asked, "What's your name, your real name."

"I go by Scorpion, just Scorpion."

At that moment I thought that was odd, but didn't attach much importance to his response. I figured he was an individualist more so than others and had created a persona that fit his lifestyle. However, after some discussion and telling Scorpion I had a book he should read, he gave me his actual name and address so I could drop the book off at his house.

During my moments on the air for this show I talked about the movie *We Were Soldiers Once, and Young*, and what a realistic portrayal of the Vietnam War it presented, although the producers bent the ending significantly. After viewing the movie's premiere, General Hal Moore, then Lieutenant Colonel, said, "This time Hollywood got it right."

Off the air, I spoke with Scorpion. It was one of those one-sided conversations during which Scorpion did most of the answering. He regaled me about his exploits as a highly decorated Navy SEAL. He told me he was a sniper with one hundred eighty-three confirmed kills, including a renegade Russian major in Bangkok, and a Russian diplomat in Moscow. Scorpion spoke of his awards, the Silver Star and Purple Heart, when a Vietnamese papasan sliced his gut open with a machete. He told me about missions in Cambodia, along the Ho Chi Minh Trail, and Laos, and said he had taken part in top secret missions in North Vietnam and China, and with the Phoenix Program.

During our discussions, I naturally asked about places and times to establish a reference to compare our tours of duty. Scorpion told me he worked out of Nha Trang for many of his covert border crossings into Cambodia.

I told him I was familiar with Nha Trang and Ban Me Thuot. Scorpion said he didn't know Ban Me Thuot—and I thought, *how odd, since helicopters would have staged from that airfield, or at least refueled there during his missions*. Again, I attached little importance to Scorpion's lack of II Corps geographical knowledge.

After more discussion, Scorpion told me he had placed his medals and SEAL Trident in his mother's coffin just before her burial. Now that struck me as very strange, especially him parting with his Trident. I had raised my antennae.

When we talked about the GI Bill, Scorpion said he graduated from college with a degree in psychology after being discharged as a lieutenant in the Navy. I knew naval officers needed a college degree prior to receiving their commissions and wondered how Scorpion had done things in reverse. Also, when Lynn introduced Scorpion on the air, he said he was a Navy SEAL but would not speak again about his service.

Lynn asked for our impressions and opinions of Operation Iraqi Freedom. Josh explained how the military was doing many positive things for the Iraqi people and that they appreciated the American military's presence. Lynn asked us how we felt about politicians and regular citizens speaking anti-war sentiments.

All the vets in the booth were adamantly in agreement when I said, "We're still at war and too many people have already forgotten that and September 11th. You cannot tell me that terrorism and Saddam Hussein are not connected somewhere and in one way or another. We must support our troops until they complete their missions. Every time someone mouths off, the enemy becomes emboldened and wants to fight on. There's nothing wrong with expressing one's opinion, but whatever happened to discretion?"

The best part of this show was telling the story of reuniting with Randy after thirty years and how Lynn played "Spirit in the Sky" for him as he drove away from Canfield. That Randy had reacted so emotionally, that he had to pull over when he started crying, genuinely surprised Lynn. "Now that's a special request that will be difficult to beat," I said.

As she had done before, Lynn ended this veterans' show with "We Gotta Get out of This Place" by the Animals. Then all of us went our separate ways. I thanked Lynn, telling her she was every veteran's best friend.

Afterwards I thought all about the show, especially Scorpion's Navy SEAL stories. As I rehashed those tales, I became agitated by the discrepancies that had laced Scorpion's stories but eventually did not give them another thought until …

"Not yet dry behind the ears, not old enough to buy a beer, but old enough to die for his country.

He can recite to you the nomenclature of a machine gun or grenade launcher and use either one effectively if he must.

He digs foxholes and latrines and can apply first aid like a professional

He can march until he is told to stop, or stop until he is told to march.

He obeys orders instantly and without hesitation, but he is not without spirit or individual dignity. He is self-sufficient.

... He sometimes forgets to brush his teeth, but never to clean his rifle. He can cook his own meals, mend his own clothes, and fix his own hurts.

If you're thirsty, he'll share his water with you; if you are hungry, food. He'll even split his ammunition with you in the midst of battle when you run low.

He has learned to use his hands like weapons and weapons like they were his hands.

He can save your life-or take it, because that is his job. He will often do twice the work of a civilian, draw half the pay, and still find ironic humor in it all. He has seen more suffering and death than he should have in his short lifetime. He has wept in public and in private, for friends who have fallen in combat and is unashamed.

He feels every note of the National Anthem vibrate through his body while at rigid attention, while tempering the burning desire to 'square-away' those around him who haven't bothered to stand, remove their hat, or even stop talking.

... Just as did his father, grandfather, and great-grandfather, he is paying the price for our freedom. Beardless or not, he is not a boy. He is the American Fighting Man that has kept this country free for over two hundred years.

He has asked nothing in return, except our friendship and understanding.
Remember him, always, for he has earned our respect and admiration with his blood.
And now we have women over there in danger, doing their part in this tradition of going to war when our nation calls us to do so.
As you go to bed tonight, remember this. A short lull, a little shade, and a picture of loved ones in their helmets."

—Sarah Palin, *America by Heart: Reflections on Family, Faith, and Flag,* Harper, 2010

December 2004: Stolen Valor

…. until I read the book, *Stolen Valor*, by B.G. Burkett, a Vietnam veteran.

This book exposed the many myths about Vietnam and set the record straight. It shed light on how the government, the media, and Hollywood had stereotyped the Vietnam vet—even the VA and some veterans themselves. The amount of information in the book was overwhelming, especially the stories about all the phonies claiming to be highly decorated veterans of the Vietnam War.

The book mesmerized me, and then; it hit me. As Burkett told story after story about phonies, I realized I could have been reading about Scorpion! He fit the author's profile of a phony; slovenly, supposedly a former elite warrior and trained killer, never at a loss for words or an unbelievable war story with a dash of mystery. I recalled Scorpion's stories from the Y-103 studio and re-examined their discrepancies. Scorpion was a goddamned phony! I was sure of it.

I told some friends about the encounter with Scorpion and the book, *Stolen Valor*. One of those guys, Jack, suggested I go online to a website to confirm or debunk Scorpion's claim of being a SEAL. I did so and wrote to the author. Burkett never wrote back to me, but he forwarded my letter to a friend. I'll call Burkett's friend, Commander Grant, who had been a member of the command structure at the Navy's training facility for SEALs at Coronado, California.

Grant confirmed my suspicions. Every story Scorpion had told was untrue or taken from books or movies, another typical tactic used by phony veterans. Grant told me that SEALS never interdicted the Ho Chi Minh Trail, nor did they operate in North Vietnam and China. It was ludicrous that any SEAL would assassinate anyone in Bangkok or Moscow. Scorpion had latched onto every self-indulging angle to build up his prowess as an elite, covert warrior.

Grant and I spoke on the telephone two or three times. He wanted to expose Scorpion. He wanted to set up a sting operation involving the local press, with cameras—the works. I sent Grant all the information I had, but all for naught— Scorpion was elusive and his email and phone numbers no longer worked.

I contacted Lynn Davis at Y-103 and presented my story and evidence. We discussed next year's show, and I hoped Scorpion would not be a part of it. That bastard had created an awkward situation for everyone—me, Lynn, the radio station. So, I decided I would not jeopardize Lynn's show. I would confront Scorpion in a way to keep Lynn clear of any confrontation.

During one conversation I got choked up—something from Vietnam triggered that reaction. Lynn said, "This is really bothering you."

"Yeah, when I think about everything my buddies went through and then some son of a bitch like Scorpion comes along, it's easy to get pissed ... then emotional."

***

In 2013, Congress passed the "Stolen Valor Act" which made it a federal offense to make false claims about receiving or wearing military awards.

"From ancient times and into the Middle Ages, man had dreamed of taking to the sky, of soaring into the blue like the birds. One savant in Spain in the year 875 is known to have covered himself with feathers in the attempt. Others devised wings of their own design and jumped from rooftops and towers—some to their deaths—in Constantinople, Nuremberg, Perugia. Learned monks conceived schemes on paper. And starting about 1490, Leonardo da Vinci made the most serious studies. He felt predestined to study flight, he said, and related a childhood memory of a kite flying down onto his cradle. According to brothers Wilbur and Orville Wright of Dayton, Ohio, it began for them with a toy from France, a small helicopter brought home by their father, Bishop Milton Wright, a great believer in the educational value of toys. The creation of a French experimenter of the nineteenth century, Alphonse Pénaud, it was little more than a stick with twin propellers and twisted rubber bands, and probably cost 50 cents. "Look here, boys," said the Bishop, something concealed in his hands. When he let go it flew to the ceiling. They called it the "bat." Orville's first teacher in grade school, Ida Palmer, would remember him at his desk tinkering with bits of wood. Asked what he was up to, he told her he was making a machine of a kind that he and his brother were going to fly someday."

—David McCullough, *The Wright Brothers,* Simon & Schuster, 2015

June 2005: Four Masher Aircraft Commanders—Band of Brothers, Part 5

I drove to Randy's home in Wallingford, Pennsylvania, just outside of Philadelphia, for a three-day mini-reunion with four Mashers. Randy and I greeted each other just like the previous year, then settled in his fifth-floor condominium.

The next day we went to a helicopter museum in Franklin, Pennsylvania. Later that afternoon Captain Richard Cross, Tricky Dick, joined us at Randy's place. Tricky was a Bravo Good Dealer for just a few months in the autumn of 1970 before being transferred to A Troop of the 1st of the 9th in the 1st Cav. He was on his second tour and wanted to fly scouts again, so Mr. Clean accommodated his transfer.

We got in Randy's jeep and drove to "Old Town" Philadelphia where Lou Bartolotta, Masher 2-7, the Godfather, lived with his wife, Esme. The couple lived in a condo, converted from an 1850 warehouse on the edge of Philadelphia's historical downtown. They lived about six blocks from Independence Hall and Betsy Ross's house. Wow! You could smell the history!

In a light rain, Lou greeted us on his porch. He was the same old, crazy Lou. We hugged and looked at each other, nodded approval, and went up the elevator to his condo.

After Vietnam, Lou went to Embry-Riddle University in Daytona, Florida, and earned his bachelor's degree in Professional Aeronautics—then things took off for him. He eventually got a job flying for Bell-Agusta helicopters, which would later become Agusta-Westland Helicopters. He advanced quickly and soon became one of that company's top officials flying all over the world, making deals with huge industries and foreign governments. One month earlier he was in Beijing, China, meeting with that country's Minister of Trade—not bad for a former Army warrant officer and slick driver.

After I met Esme, the four of us former Army aviators got comfortable in Lou's den and talked about Nam and each other's lives. I had pictures, and we looked through them recalling this, that, and the other things. One picture drew particular attention from Lou. It was a picture I took of four Masher birds in an echelon left formation. I told Lou that I vividly remembered the day I took the picture because Lou was being an asshole.

"What?" said Lou, "Me, an asshole!"

"Roger that. Allow me to refresh your memory."

I was Yellow 1, leading a flight of six Masher Hueys. We were flying south, along the coast, back to Tuy Hoa. I called for echelon left so I could take some cool pictures of a nice tight formation as viewed from my left seat. But Lou and Fish were goofing off—being assholes, and refused to get into the new formation. Instead, Lou and Fish were floating around behind the formation, pretending to be Charlie-Model gunships, covering the flight. But Lou eventually accommodated me, resulting in the picture.

Masher Reunion; the author (Jo3y and Masher 2-4), Randy (Moleman and Masher 2-2) Clark, Richard (Tricky Dick and Masher 3) Cross, and Lou (The Godfather and Masher 2-7) Bartolotta (Author's private collection).

After sharing more war stories, some beginning with, *this is no shit.* Lou led us to a restaurant. Before beginning our meal, we lifted our glasses and toasted Bravo 227, "To Bravo 227 and those of us who survived … and to the memory of those who did not."

"Hear, hear," all answered, and I'm sure Lieutenants Dyer and Douglas, Captain Head and Specialist Burgess came to mind. It was a fitting way to begin the meal.

Afterwards we returned to Lou's and made our goodbyes. Lou demanded that we get together as frequently as possible. "No more of this thirty-year stuff," he said. So, we all agreed and planned to meet in Washington DC in July 2006 for the next VHPA reunion.

Randy, Tricky, and I returned to Wallingford. Tricky drove home and I spent the night in Randy's condo. The next day we drove to Washington to tour the new flight museum and to visit the Wall. Going to the wall worried me, because of my previous loss of composure, so I put Randy on alert. But, much to my relief, I was fine when we walked the Wall and found the names of classmates Butch Sears and Jeff Coffin; and our Bravo Good Dealers.

We also visited the Smithsonian Museum of American History, which displayed a Huey and other Vietnam War exhibits. It had been a long day, made even longer by a ninety-eight-degree temperature and humidity at eighty percent. My ass was dragging and my back was killing me. Randy kept an eye on me, thinking I might pass out.

On the following morning, Randy and I said goodbye, and I drove home, more excited than ever before about going to a reunion of the VHPA.

***

I sent a copy of the infamous picture to Lou. He had it framed and proudly displayed it on the desk in his office.

Doug Bradley and Craig Werner have compiled a list of songs they consider as the top-ten during the Vietnam War. The number-one song is:

1. "We Gotta Get Out of This Place" by The Animals.

"No one saw this coming. Not the writers of the song — the dynamic Brill Building duo of Barry Mann and Cynthia Weil; not the group who recorded it — The Animals and their iconic lead singer, Eric Burdon; not the 3 million soldiers who fought in Vietnam who placed extra importance on the lyrics... Or as Leroy Tecube, an Apache infantryman stationed south of Chu Lai in 1968, recalls: 'When the chorus began, singing ability didn't matter; drunk or sober, everyone joined in as loud as he could.' No wonder it became the title of our book!"

—Doug Bradley, "A Veterans's Playlist: The Top 10 Vietnam War Songs," from "Remembering Vietnam Special Report," 10 November 2015, nextavenue.org

—Doug Bradley and Craig Werner, *We Gotta Get Out of This Place: The Soundtrack of the Vietnam War (Culture and Politics in the Cold War and Beyond,* University of Massachusetts Press, 21 October 2015

9 November 2005: Fifth Appearance on Y-103

My fifth appearance on Lynn Davis's Veterans Day show involved a change in format and venue. This time Lynn's usual crew of veterans assembled at a local restaurant. My friend, Jack, was there also to enjoy the afternoon and to help me confront that lying fake, Scorpion. Those in attendance were Monty and Jim, Tom and Dave from the Air Force reserve, along with me and Jack.

Lynn introduced me to her listeners and expressed herself unexpectantly—even though she knew about my service—it amazed her that I actually flew helicopters. I thought she was struggling for words and helped her out as best I could with my answer, speaking about just doing my job as an Army aviator, no matter what set of circumstances came my way.

The show went well, but I found the remote locale uncomfortable and chaotic. I missed a good deal of the show simply because I couldn't hear the music and other interviews Lynn conducted.

Prior to the show, I spoke with Lynn about the Scorpion situation. We were both hoping he wouldn't show, but he did, quite early as a matter of fact.

Considering all factors, I told Lynn that I would do nothing to upset or disrupt her show. But when we were off the air, the gloves were coming off and Scorpion was going down.

Since Scorpion was so early, I purposely sat next to him and asked him question after question about his supposed service as a Navy SEAL in Vietnam. He lied answer after answer, even contradicting himself from lies I recalled from last year's show. I was ready for the showdown.

After Lynn closed the show, I asked Scorpion to join me and Jack at our table. When he sat down, I wasted no time and told him he was no SEAL and for him to continue to lie was an insult to all real SEALs and dishonored all who served in Vietnam. Scorpion remained unflappable, sticking to his stories even when I countered every lie with information I had gathered from other *real* SEALs.

I spoke about and referred to the book, *Stolen Valor*, to help show Scorpion was a liar. For example, I said, "Scorpion, an hour ago you told me received the Navy Cross in Nam."

"Yeah, for pulling Marines out of a firefight."

"That's bullshit!" I opened *Stolen Valor* to the reference section to a list of all Navy Cross recipients. "Look, your name isn't here."

"That must be a mistake."

"You're no SEAL! That's why it's not here," I said and quickly threw another question at him. "What's your BUD/S number?"

BUD/S was the Navy's acronym for Basic Underwater Demolition SEALS training. A SEAL's BUD?S number is comparable to a WOC's flight school number— something that is *never ... never* forgotten.

Scorpion hesitated, hemmed and hawed and said, "I can't remember ... sixty-eight something."

"No way you'd forget your BUD/S number. That's something a SEAL would never forget. And hear this—the SEALs at Coronado, the training facility for SEALS, never heard of you!"

"I have my DD214, orders, papers, all that stuff at home," continued the liar. "I'll show you—bring them next year."

"If by some stretch of the imagination you are a SEAL, I'll be the first to apologize," I said. "But that won't happen because you're a phony and those papers, if they do exist, are phony too. They never heard of you at Coronado, and they have records on every underwater demolition trainee since the 1940s."

The more we spoke, the less convincing Scorpion became. I had made my point and backed it up and exposed at least ten lies. I ended the conversation by telling him again to not dishonor those who really served—to stop lying. Then Jack and I left the restaurant.

Jack made an interesting observation as we walked through the parking lot. "You know, Joe, if I were a SEAL and someone challenged my service, my integrity, I'd really be pissed off! That bastard sat there as cool as could be and took everything you threw at him. No way he's a SEAL."

Two weeks later, I received two letters. The letter from the SEALs training base at Coronado, California, confirmed that Scorpion never was a SEAL. The other letter, from the military records branch in St. Louis, showed that no record of service existed on Scorpion—the liar wasn't even in the Navy!

I took copies of the letters to Y-103 and met with Lynn. "You can't let that bastard back on the show. It's not right," I said. "Look at these letters."

Understandably, Lynn was uncomfortable with the whole predicament and made no commitment about next year's show. I even told her to drop me if she thought it would be for the best.

Lynn said, "I can't do that. You bring so much to the show."

Hearing Lynn's comments surprised me.

"Your stories are great … and they're relevant … important, and they're not just me-me-me stories—they're fascinating and the listeners enjoy them. I know because they've told me. I get all kinds of calls and messages."

Hearing Lynn's comment made me feel very good about my PTSD-afflicted self. I thanked her but told her that the whole Scorpion thing left a nasty taste in my mouth, and probably everyone else's as well "How could something so positive, so neat for you and the vets become a problem? I don't need this, don't need another confrontation. But I couldn't let that damn liar dishonor real vets any longer. I hope you understand."

Lynn understood how the whole thing had affected me and how passionate I was about the issue.

***

Jack later heard from reliable sources that someone else had confronted Scorpion about his lying and impersonating a veteran. Since our encounter at the restaurant, no one I know has heard from Scorpion, nor has he called the radio station.

This was the last show during which veterans were a part of the format in the studio or at a remote location. In talking with Lynn, I deduced that was a management decision. Lynn would return to her basic format of taking calls but still making the day as special as possible—and her success continued. Lynn's Veterans Day show remains the most popular show of the year, just as she remains every veteran's best friend. What a lady!

** PTSD **

137

"Our past may explain why we're suffering but we must not use it as an excuse to stay in bondage."

—Joyce Meyer, *Battlefield of the Mind: Winning the Battle in Your Mind*, Warner Faith; Revised edition, October 2002

"We are products of our past, but we don't have to be prisoners of it."

—Rick Warren, *The Purpose Driven Life: What on Earth Am I Here for?,* Zondervan; 10th Anniversary edition, December 2013

Part 8

Transformations

I'm not crazy, I was abused.

I'm not shy, I'm protecting myself.

I'm not bitter, I'm speaking the truth.

I'm not hanging onto the past, I've been damaged.

I'm not delusional, I lived a nightmare.

I'm not weak, I was trusting.

I'm not giving up, I'm healing.

I'm not incapable of love, I'm giving.

I'm not alone, I see you all here.

I'm fighting this.

—Rene Smith, declutteryourmind.com

February 2006: Getting Help—PTSD, Part 11

Things weren't right at home, nor on the job, and life situations were worsening. I found my old pamphlet about Vietnam vets and PTSD, looked it over, and this time realized that so many of the behaviors associated with PTSD applied to me. I called the VA clinic for a mental evaluation with Dr. Thomas Mako.

After initial interviews and a battery of testing, Dr. Mako reported to me. "Joe, not only do you have PTSD, you have severe PTSD."

I waited a handful of quiet seconds. "Doc, that's good news. Now I know what the problem is and with your help I can address that problem."

Long story, short, over the next thirteen years I was fortunate to be the patient of three marvelous psychologists: Patty Karpenko, Thomas Mako, and Mary Ann

Echols. During the lowest moments of those years, I was reminded several times by the good doctors, "Joe, you did three, combat tours … not one … three! You have many triggers and a lot of issues to deal with."

So, my professionals and I went about addressing those issues: anger, anxiety in crowds, black and white thought processes versus shades of gray, demon dreams, emotional numbness, hyper-arousal, intrusive memories, mistrust of and confrontations with authority, and survivor's guilt. Yes, there was so much more behind the fact that I cried every time I heard "Taps" played.

** PTSD **

"PTSD happens when symptoms we all experience following a trauma just don't go away."

—Dr. Carolyn Allard, Clinical Psychologist, "More PTSD Basics," from the US Department of Veterans Affairs; National Center for PTSD, 8 June 2020

It doesn't take a hero to order men into battle. It takes a hero to be one of those men who goes into battle.

—Norman Schwarzkopf

2 April 2006: Mike Novosel Died Today

CW2 Mike Novosel received the Congressional Medal of Honor for heroism as a helicopter pilot in Vietnam in October 1969. I had the honor and pleasure of meeting him and flying with him while assigned to the 5th Special Forces Flight Detachment at Fort Bragg, North Carolina.

According to his obituary, Mike flew for two tours in Vietnam as a Dustoff pilot. He logged over 2,500 hours and evacuated nearly 5,600 injured soldiers.

Two stranger-than-truth stories are worth mentioning. Mike's son, also a warrant officer, was a Dustoff pilot flying in the same AO as his dad. During their coinciding tours of duty, each was shot down … and rescued by the other!

Mike was also a veteran of World War II, flying B-24 Liberators and B-29 Super Fortresses. CW4 Mike Novosel was buried at Arlington National Cemetery on 13 April 2006. God bless Mike Novosel!

Medal of Honor recipient, Chief Warrant Officer Mike Novosel (Wikimedia Commons, public domain).

11 July 1995: President Bill Clinton announced that diplomatic relations between the USA and the Socialist Republic of Vietnam were now normalized.

It was wrong of the US to invade Vietnam ...The US lost the war because it didn't understand Vietnam ... We knew right from the outset that we would triumph ...The word 'fear' never exists in our military philosophies.

—Vo Nguyen Giap, 1995

When the last Blackhawk helicopter goes to the boneyard, it will be on a sling under a Huey.

—Pilotfriend, "Aviation Humor"

July 2006: VHPA Reunion, Washington DC— Band of Brothers, Part 6

The Vietnam Helicopters Pilot Association held its annual reunion in Washington DC, and for the first time I attended that gathering. It was an experience I enjoyed and valued immensely.

I checked in at the Marriot Hotel, just west of downtown DC, where fifteen hundred pilots and family members were gathering. Once I got settled in my room, I went to the atrium to reunite with guys, some I hadn't seen in years—in decades. Among my band of brothers were Lou Bartolotta, Randy Clark, John Goosman, and Herbie Nagel. I found it interesting how everyone still called me Joey.

We hugged, smiled and got choked up a few times while talking and reminiscing until midnight. Many of our comments began with, "Hey, do you remember ..." or "Hey, who was the guy that ..." Somebody always had an answer or could fill in the blanks.

Eventually, the conversation went to Mr. Clean, Major Harold Fisher, our CO. No one had heard from him since he left his command of the Bravo Good Deal in February 1971. And to a man, all agreed that he was the best CO any of us had ever served with—we loved that big, bald guy.

The event also reunited me with John Goosman, the gunner that survived a shoot-down on the last day of the Cambodian incursion. I could see that John's experiences in Nam still troubled him. With his permission, I briefly described how helpful my counseling at the VA had been. I urged him to try it.

John vividly recalled the two of us watching the Cobra gunship lose its rotor blade to enemy .51 cal fire and crash. During subsequent conversations we got each other caught up on our own lives. I was happy that John was a successful businessman in the Los Angeles area of California and happily married with kids.

The author with Captain Larry Winters, reunited thirty-six years after being shot down at LZ Margaret (Author's private collection).

The author with Bravo, 227, door gunner, John Goosman (Author's private collection).

At the second night's gathering, I was reunited with Captain Larry Winters. Larry was my AC when we were shot down in 083 on 18 April 1970. We embraced and immediately went about recalling and discussing the incident. It was nice to know that my memory of the shoot-down was still intact.

Captain Winters also described how he was wounded, which occurred three weeks later in Cambodia during a combat assault. It was 9 May 1970, just three weeks after our shoot-down. I had been flying that day, but not with the Yellow Flight, and by monitoring the radios listened to the incident unfold with some very tense moments.

While landing to a ridgeline LZ, without gunship cover, Captain Winters was shot through the foot by one bullet that then ricocheted off his chicken-plate, split his helmet's visor, and tore through the top of the helmet. A second bullet entered his left armpit, hit his lung, and exited through his back. He was told that over fifty AK-47 rounds had hit his aircraft, and that he was the only crew member to be wounded. His Charlie Pop, WO1 Charlie "Ratso" Bauer, did an outstanding job of getting the bird back to the PZ (Preparation Zone).

On the following day I strolled through the vendors' room where books, patches and pins, and other memorabilia for sale. I approached the tables of Joe Kline, an internationally renowned aviation artist. I stopped dead in my tracks when I saw one of his prints entitled "God's Own Lunatics." The print depicted a single Huey landing to a grassy LZ to extract a LRRP team in contact with the enemy. My own LRRP extraction in a grassy LZ immediately flooded my mind. It was as though the artist captured my incident on his canvas—so powerful was the attraction at the moment.

I spoke with Joe and told him of my unbelievable moment, and of course, bought one of his prints, which he personalized for me. He painted Bravo 227 markings on the bird along with a Cav patch on the tail, under the butt number 391. He printed Jo3y with a backward E on my seat's armor plate and Joey, the *Dennis the Menace* comic strip character, on the fuselage. The print is now displayed prominently in my workroom.

Mashers from 1969 to 1970; Larry Winters, Herbie Nagel, Larry Wilson, Bill Tritt, John Goosman, Lou Bartolotta, the author, and Randy Clark (Author's private collection).

On the next day, pilots toured Arlington National Cemetery, followed by a visit to the Wall, the Vietnam War Memorial During and a wreath-laying ceremony. Tears streamed down the faces of many pilots, including my own, during the ceremony and a brief eulogy. Then a three-ship fly-by of Blackhawks with thumping rotor blades pounded every heart, causing another release of tears. It was one of the most moving events I had ever experienced.

During the following afternoon, the Bravo 227 pilots held a mini-reunion in one of the conference rooms. I met pilots who flew with the Good Deal in 1966 through 1970, guys who started it all for the rest of us, guys who developed tactics that were passed on to us, that saved our lives and allowed us to accomplish our missions.

On July 3rd, we finally got our parade. Pilots and their families gathered near the Smithsonian Air and Space Museum for our long-overdue welcome home that would proceed right down Constitution Avenue. The humidity was high that afternoon and the temperature was in the nineties, so bottles of water made available to us. I don't know how far we marched or how long it took—I was living in the moment, savoring the cheers and the handshakes. It was also a grueling experience with the heat and my back pain, but I made it to the end—finally, the USA welcomed us back from Vietnam!

That evening, we attended a formal dinner. The most moving moment was the salute to our "Missing Man," a moment to remember all the pilots and crewmen who didn't make it back alive from Vietnam, Cambodia, and Laos.

A delicious, sit-down dinner followed.

The next morning, after goodbyes, I drove home. In route, I decided to attend another reunion of the VHPA that would take place in 2009 in Philadelphia.

The goal of PTSD counseling is to help the patient learn how to recognize the disorder, understand how it affects one's life, then learn how to deal with it, thus improving the quality of one's life. The goal of the counseled individual is to apply that information. I know—I have lived and continue to live it.

—Masher 2-4

November 2006: Group Counseling—PTSD, Part 12

Teaching remained a difficult endeavor for me, and the shit hit the fan with the Board of Education in the spring of 2006—I received termination papers at my house.

I had been experiencing a horrendous year at my junior-high building. It had become clear, and I suspected that administrative personnel and at least one member of the Board of Education wanted to fire me. I called my union for legal representation. Of course, we were going to fight this. But I was told that the Board had yet to return my lawyer's phone calls. Hell, we didn't even know what charges had or would be brought against me and by whom. That stunk! I wanted answers.

So, while my attorney did his job, I made some purposeful statements in the teachers' lounge. Word of my impending termination had already spread, and it was now time for *my* message to be spread. So, during lunch and in front of two people I knew would run to the office to huddle with an administrator to report my words, I said, "I'm not worried. The Board's tried four times to fire me and failed four times. When all is said and done, this time the Board is going to write me a check for at least six figures. Then, I'm going after the administrator, a couple of board members and the superintendent. They better have their checkbooks ready because they'll be writing checks for seven figures."

That evening, my attorney called to inform me that the Board's lawyer wanted to meet to discuss the situation. Word travels fast—doesn't it?

Negotiations ran throughout the rest of the 2005-2006 school year and into the summer. The Board got their way, getting me out of the classroom and assigning me to the downtown offices of the Board—with an assignment that would involve writing reports.

Other than the nebulous charges of racism and incompetence, my attorney and I never learned of specific charges and who brought them. Also, I reluctantly agreed to a forced retirement, effective 28 February 2009, bottom line being—the Board wanted me out of the classroom and I wanted out of their screwed-up system.

***

In January 2007, Dr. Mako officially diagnosed me with severe PTSD. During that time, Dr. Mako suggested that I also began group counseling. I was reluctant because of my earlier experience with guys like Captain Jacket and Brewski—no way would I subject myself to such encounters again. Dr. Mako assured me that his group would be remain structured, following a syllabus of instruction with objectives, not bullshit sessions.

So, after seven months of counseling, and Mako's gentle application of pressure, I agreed as long as my weekly, one-on-one sessions with him would continue. And so, I was about to begin a new journey of self-discovery and healing filled with epiphanies upon epiphanies about life and PTSD.

For the next three years, I met with a new band of brothers, Dr. Mako's PTSD group. We met at the Youngstown VA clinic for three hours every Monday morning. We shared our traumas, console and encourage each other, cry and hug … and laugh— then come to forgive ourselves to for things we had less control over than we had believed. That was a tough one for me—forgiving others and myself.

At the end of each eighteen-month cycle, each participant spoke for one entire three-hour session, telling his story. During my session, I spoke about my triggers; including the decapitated soldier, the day that the .51 cal opened up on the Yellow Flight and miraculously hit no one or nothing, and the death of the little girl. I got through it, in a matter-of-factly way with no display of emotion. I didn't realize that I approached the task as a lesson, as I would in a classroom, but with some degree of a foxhole mentality.

During my next one-on-one session with Dr. Mako, a few days later, he suggested I repeat the eighteen-month group cycle. He thought I was still burying a significant amount of emotion—still reluctant to face my demons. He used my presentation to the group as an example, which enlightened me—an aha moment. So, I agreed and completed another eighteen-month cycle. Then, at the end of the second cycle, I again spoke about my three tours. This time, I didn't hold back—cried and just let it all out.

Two beautiful moments occurred during my *release*. After retelling the story about the death of the little girl, one of the more hard-nosed Vietnam vets, stood up and walked right up to me. He wrapped his arms around me and gave me a big hug, a genuine, warm, big hug. He said it took balls to stand up to Wilk, telling him I would not lie about the crew chief hurling flare fuses at the civilians. "You did the right thing, man. That took balls," he said as I cried. "You have guts."

Moments later, Paul, another vet who had grown quite close to me and who had a similar incident involving the death of four innocent civilians, said, "You're okay, Joe. And, you know what? When you die and go to heaven, that little girl is going to be standing next to St. Peter. She'll be smiling and she'll give you a hug and tell you, 'It's okay—you did fine.'"

I came to understand why I thought and acted the way I did in all aspects of my life. That was difficult, and even more difficult—not beating myself up for that behavior. Such was the effect of three combat tours and how they profoundly defined my PTSD.

** PTSD **

"There is clear evidence from internal investigations in the past that some raters actually see themselves as adversaries to veterans. If a claim can be minimized, then the government has saved money, regardless of the need of the veteran. Just recently, the press exposed an official e-mail from a high-level staff person who stated in essence that PTSD diagnosis was becoming too prevalent and offered ways to delay and deflect ratings in order to save the government money."

—Taylor Armstrong, *Hiding from Reality: My Story of Love, Loss, and Finding the Courage Within,* 2012, Gallery Books

"The Army might screw you and your girlfriend might dump you and the enemy might kill you, but the shared commitment to safeguard one another's lives is unnegotiable and only deepens with time. The willingness to die for another person is a form of love that even religions fail to inspire, and the experience of it changes a person profoundly."

—Sebastian Junger, *War*, published by Twelve, 2010

6 July 2007: At Mott's Military Museum with Randy Clark—Band of Brothers, Part 7

Thirty years ago, today, Randy and I pulled the medevac during which we chopped

bamboo with the rotor blades to reach a wounded soldier. Randy was the AC, and I was his Charlie Pop. Today, I was the AC and Randy was the Charlie Pop as I picked him up at his Columbus hotel and drove to Mott's Military Museum in Groveport, Ohio.

During the ride, I told Randy about the death of Dao Tran. He had never heard all the details. He also informed me that Wilk was

The author and Randy Clark pose by 048 at Motts Military Museum in Groveport, Ohio (Author's private collection).

now the chief helicopter pilot for a large company on the East Coast. I found that upsetting, but I thought it fit Wilk's personality.

Upon our arrival at the museum Warren greeted us in his own exuberant way and before we knew it, we were standing next to 048. Randy told me he felt the same emotions as I had when I first saw 048 in August 2000. Warren unlocked our bird, and we crawled all over her.

We took dozens of pictures and explored the bird again, almost like a preflight. Then Eldon Erlenback approached and Warren introduced him to us.

Eldon was carrying a binder filled with pictures and papers from his tour of duty with the 5th Battalion of the 7th Cavalry, 1st Air Cavalry Division. He was in Nam when we were and experienced many of the same events as Randy and me. Most notably, he lived at FSB Snuffy for a few months and was on Shakey's Hill, in the same company as Skytrooper Shakey, the firebase's namesake.

Somewhere during the conversation Eldon asked me if I knew anything about two pilots getting killed at Snuffy when a grunt's M-16 accidentally discharged. A chill ran through my body. "Eldon, I was at Snuffy getting ready for a CA when someone discharged an M-16 in the Huey right next to me."

After thirty-seven years, I was again experiencing one of those incredible chance meetings. Unknowingly Eldon's and my path crossed at FSB Snuffy in Vietnam in 1970.

"The AC was Cuddles, CW2 John Codling. He reported the incident over the radio and climbed out of his bird. I went over to help him as a medic rushed to his side."

"I was next to the guy whose weapon discharged," said Eldon. "He was a new guy in my squad and I told him to safety his weapon. Wouldn't you know it—the damn thing went off."

"Holy shit! We had to be standing less than ten feet from each other. That's incredible! I mean, here we are today talking about that incident—putting it all together."

Warren didn't believe what was happening, what he was hearing. He had witnessed impromptu or unexpected reunions before, but he was blown away by the immediacy and intensity of this unfolding three-way reunion.

Eldon showed me an account of the accident in the 5th of the 7th's journal. Inaccuracies abounded, the most apparent being two pilots were killed. "They weren't killed. Only one, CW2 John Codling, Cuddles, was wounded in the elbow."

For all these years, Eldon and the 5th of the 7th thought much more damage had occurred—and I can understand why. Immediately after the weapon discharged, Eldon muscled his new-guy grunt out of the bird. At that time, he knew at least one pilot had been hit, but not to what extent.

"I assure you, Eldon, Cuddles was the only pilot hit. The M-16 round shattered a tie-down ring on the cargo deck and shrapnel pierced Cuddles in his elbow." I showed Eldon one of the tie-down rings on 048's cargo deck.

"Damn, for all these years we thought the two pilots got killed," said Eldon.

"Nope, not at all. The last I heard, Cuddles is alive and well somewhere in Nebraska."

The conversation shifted to Randy and Eldon and Shakey's Hill. Warren pulled me aside—he had a story to share with me.

"Joey, I want you to hear this. I'll never forget the time you were here with your daughter. She sat in the left seat of your helicopter and I was in the right seat. After you explained things to both of us, you climbed out the cargo door. This look came over her face. I'll never forget it." Warren as his voice trembled.

Warren told me Jackie said. "'I just realized something,' she said, 'I'm twenty years old and when my Dad was twenty, he was flying this very helicopter in a war!'"

"Can you imagine the responsibility he carried as a kid the same age as you?" asked Warren.

"That's what I mean," said Jackie. "Can you imagine?"

Warren told me that got to him and choked him up—and with this, his retelling of his encounter with Jackie, he became choked up again and tears crept down his cheeks.

"Warren," I said, "that conversation happened because of you and your museum. Your primary reason for presenting your memorabilia is to connect the objects with actual people. You succeeded with my daughter and I'm sure you've succeeded with many, many more visitors." I got emotional and added, "For the first time in Jackie's life she connected with me in a very special way."

Warren wiped away his tears, and we embraced. "You're a special guy, Warren. You keep on doing what you're doing because it's working—people are connecting. Look at Eldon connecting with Randy and me, and 048—amazing!"

"I had to share that with you, Joey. It hit home with me. I'll never forget her sitting in that helicopter, just like you did all those years ago in Vietnam."

Warren then described how he saw Jackie—a young college student in her own environment with her set of priorities and responsibilities compared to mine at the same age, flying this helicopter in Vietnam.

"Thanks for sharing that with me, Warren. I had no idea."

Randy and Eldon joined us, and Randy asked if he could climb onto 048's topside.

"Of course, you guys do what you want—it's your helicopter."

Randy made his way to the Huey's top, and I followed—much more slowly than in 1970, but we made it. We checked out the rotor head and reminisced some more, posed for pictures, then climbed down. It wasn't easy for me, and I thought I might lose my balance and hurt myself. When I reached the ground I said to Warren, "That's the last time I'll ever do that," and *he* breathed a sigh of relief.

Warren took us inside to show us his Vietnam display and my corner, complete with mannequin and the memorabilia I had donated. After more pictures and discussion, I pointed to a small picture no one seemed to pay attention to. "Hey everybody, look at that picture. That's Randy standing next to a Masher helicopter."

"I'll be damned," said Randy. "How did I miss that?"

I told Randy what I remembered about taking the picture and Randy replied, "More connecting the dots."

Our last stop, to Warren's office where we watched the movie *Shakey's Hill*, which proved to be just as emotional as any other moment of our visit. Eldon enhanced the viewing with his grunt's-eye-view and drawing on personal experiences. His bit-by-bit narrative personalized the moment and didn't distract from the story at all—he knew when and when not to speak.

After viewing the movie, Randy seemed to be overwhelmed. I could tell how this experience had been affecting him—just like Eldon, Warren, and I had been touched. He used his "connecting the dots" analogy with Eldon's story.

We made our goodbyes and left the museum exhausted and emotionally drained.

***

After this day's experiences all I could think about was going back in time, to Nam and doing it all over again but this time, take it all in: do more with my flying machines, save Dao's life, deal with emotions in a timely manner, see the flight surgeon after my shoot-down, request the 58th AHC for my third tour, and look more deeply at the Vietnamese people, their customs and country.

Randy expressed similar thoughts. He also thought the day at Mott's would be one of the most memorable in his life, not only because of reuniting with 048, but for meeting Eldon and "connecting the dots" of another Nam experience. He was also very impressed with Warren and his endeavor. "You know, Joey, Warren's done it right. It's so clear he cares about his museum and everything in it."

"I felt the same way the first time I visited his place and met him."

"But the thing that got to me was how he personalized everything," continued Randy. "His museum isn't just about the artifacts—it's about the people behind the artifacts."

"Roger that." I couldn't have put it better.

** PTSD **

"Post-Traumatic Stress Disorder"

What are the symptoms of PTSD?

"Re-experiencing symptoms include: Flashbacks—reliving the trauma over and over, including physical symptoms like a racing heart or sweating; Bad dreams; and Frightening thoughts.

Re-experiencing symptoms may cause problems in a person's everyday routine. The symptoms can start from the person's own thoughts and feelings. Words, objects, or situations that are reminders of the event can also trigger re-experiencing symptoms."

—National Institute for Mental Health, "Post-Traumatic Stress Disorder," Revised May 2019, (This publication is in the public domain and may be reproduced or copied without permission from NIMH.)

July 2008: More Demon Dreams—PTSD, Part 13

The same dream that had haunted me years ago returned with a vengeance—Viet Cong were again visiting my sleep—shadowy figures standing at my bed. I remember trying to decide what to do while my heart pounded—I actually felt a pain in my chest. *The hell with it,* I thought—*I'm going down fighting.*

Still asleep, I kicked back the covers and flailed away with my fists. I swung my legs over the side of the bed and stepped toward my stalkers—and then I awoke—flat on the floor. My foot had become entangled in the sheet and I never made it to my feet—I landed on my right hand and bent my middle finger into some grotesque angle. I felt some pain, but nothing severe. I pulled my finger, shook my hand and climbed back into bed.

When I awoke a few hours later, my finger was throbbing and bent at the first knuckle nearly ninety degrees. I showered, dressed, and drove myself to the emergency room of the hospital. The x-rays revealed a detached tendon—no broken bones.

The next day I drove to Akron to see a hand specialist. The result: For the next eight months I had to wrap the finger in a plastic splint, then a brace, and finally, just tape. Slowly, ever so slowly, the tendon re-attached itself to the bone. I was thankful it healed naturally. The alternative would have been surgery with a recovery time of about six months.

The moral of the story is never detach a tendon—go for the broken bone.

***

We suspected my nightmares contributed to the state of depression I had been suffering through for several months. I had reached a point so low that I didn't care if I lived or died. I told Dr. Mako, "If I got run over by a bus—I wouldn't care—just end it all."

Dr. Mako immediately registered concern, "Joe, I have to ask you—do you want to commit suicide?"

I assured him I would never take my own life—but I cared little about living.

So, Dr. Mako and the nurse practitioner put me on medication and intensified my counseling. Slowly but surely, I climbed out of the depression and dealt with the guilt that had been troubling so very much.

** *PTSD* **

"Treatment and Therapies"

"The main treatments for people with PTSD are medications, psychotherapy ('talk' therapy), or both. Everyone is different, and PTSD affects people differently, so a treatment that works for one person may not work for another. It is important for anyone with PTSD to be treated by a mental health provider who is experienced with PTSD. Some people with PTSD may need to try different treatments to find what works for their symptoms.

...Other ongoing problems can include panic disorder, depression, substance abuse, and feeling suicidal."

"Medications"

"The most studied type of medication for treating PTSD are antidepressants, which may help control PTSD symptoms such as sadness, worry, anger, and feeling numb inside. Other medications may be helpful for treating specific PTSD symptoms, such as sleep problems and nightmares."

—National Institute for Mental Health, "Post-Traumatic Stress Disorder," Revised May 2019, (This publication is in the public domain and may be reproduced or copied without permission from NIMH.)

A layperson's definition of Sensitivity to Injustice: Relevant to anxiety and PTSD trauma and hypervigilance, an over-reaction to, or adverse reactivity to injustice or a perceived injustice.

—Masher 2-4

** PTSD **

(The following quote is appropriate for PTSD counseling and recovery.)

Recovery is a process. It takes time. It takes patience. It takes everything you've got.

—Northpoint, "Worth the Read—Seventy-five
   Meaningful and Inspiring Addiction Recovery
   Quotes"

July 2008: The Epiphany

After completing my first eighteen-month cycle of intensive group therapy, I repeated the process while continuing with one-on-one counseling with Dr. Mako. As I neared the end of the second cycle, Dr. Mako presented me with a letter from both he and Dr. Mary Ann Echols, who also took part in my treatment.

The letter outlined my progress, complimenting me on my serious approach to PTSD. It highlighted four areas that were directly related to my trauma: guilt, the need to be in control, head versus heart and emotional well-being, but of most importance, sensitivity to injustice.

During counseling sessions, we had discussed my traumas, triggers, and symptoms of PTSD deliberately and continually. However, today, after reading Drs. Mako and Echols's letter, my understanding of some factors comprising my PTSD-laced personality rose to a new height of awareness and relief, in particular, as it could apply to the Dau Tran incident. The following excerpt best explains my position.

"Hopefully, in the course of working on your trauma, you have become more aware of the effect that hindsight has on the perspective you adopt towards your war experiences. Although guilt may be connected to your war experiences, it was inflated because it was based on the irrational belief that you were 100% responsible for what happened and that somehow you had 100% control over what others did. Hopefully, the group discussions made this irrational belief clearer to you. We encourage you to accept that this was a shared event and that for many years you were likely taking on more responsibility than was rightfully yours to have. Although no one was legally held 'responsible' in your traumatic event, ironically, you actually and unfortunately blamed yourself and held yourself to be 100% responsible. This incident is suspected to have contributed to your sensitivity to any perceived 'injustice' and driven efforts to make any wrongs, right.

We are encouraged by your desire to continue attending the PTSD group. It reflects your strong desire to achieve a better peace with the past and a more hopeful future."

—Thomas Mako, Ph.D. Psychologist and Mary Ann Echols, Ph.D. Psychologist, 16 May 2008

The reason for so many of my problems with management, those figures of authority, became clearer than ever—I had a sensitivity to injustice. However, it is prudent to note that so many of those injustices manifested themselves in environments with figures of authority that perpetuated mistrust and injustice. The ways and means of such administrative practices included hypocrisy, double-talking and lying, ignoring accepted and approved policies and a *look-the-other-way* mentality, incompetence and vindictiveness, and flagrant violations of labor-management contracts.

Please recall my confrontations with university professors about wasting my class time; and later, wanting three areas of certification as opposed to two. Please recall the appalling student behavior I encountered throughout my teaching career and the lack of, or marginal support given by, administrations.

I accept my sensitivity to injustice. I welcome the enlightenment shone upon my PTSD. But that must also be qualified by the many figures of authority I encountered over the decades—those who saw me as a threat to their own public and professional images and positions, those who sugar-coated, danced around, misrepresented or refused to face issues detrimental to their institutions.

Drs. Mako and Echols nailed it: my sensitivity to injustice results from the death of the eleven-year-old girl, Dau Tran, in Vietnam.

** PTSD **

You don't have to save me—you just have to hold my hand while I save myself.

—Unknown, declutterthemind.com

"Forgiving isn't something you do for someone else. It's something you do for yourself. It's saying, 'You're not important enough to have a stranglehold on me.' It's saying, 'You don't get to trap me in the past. I am worthy of a future.'"

—Jodi Picoult, *The Storyteller*, Atria/Emily Bestler Books; Reprint edition, November 2013

Peace and Forgiveness, a gift from Aunt Theresa (Author's private collection).

Summer 2008: Confessions—PTSD, Part 14

Dr. Mako gave me an assignment; write a story about Dao Tran—one that could be a vehicle for reconciliation, forgiveness, and for releasing emotions still buried deep in my heart.

I completed that assignment, which Dr. Mako reviewed and then discussed with me. He thought the story was effective and served its purpose, although I did not experience any release of emotion during its writing. Forgiving Wilk and Dennehy, and myself had not occurred either. Honestly, I don't think I'll ever be able to do that. But it was a step toward healing and would be the catalyst for another encounter.

***

After hearing about experiences involving alienation from veterans in my PTSD group, I invited my brothers and sisters to my home to share with them, my stories about Vietnam, in particular, the stories of trauma, especially that of Dao Tran.

On a summer evening, Steve and Kathy, Eddie, Paul and Monica joined my family. To prepare for the meeting, I provided them with a factual account of the incident and the fictional story I had written—Dr. Mako's assignment.

I stumbled for words at first, then they just flowed, knowing I was doing something beneficial, not only for myself, but for everyone in the room. I also became emotional soon after the discussion began. It was nice that my brothers and sisters had read my words about Dao and had questions. It was even nicer that everyone in the room agreed that I was not totally to blame—in fact, my part of the blame was minimal, echoing opinions expressed in group counseling and the Mako-Echols letter.

I thanked them all for their perceptions, support and questions. Yes, because of counseling and hearing so many comments and opinions, I hoped to ease up on myself and recognized that I too was a victim of circumstances and that my share of the guilt was actually minimal. I just had to convince myself of that. But I hastened to explain what none of them would ever fully understand—something I would carry with me to the grave—me not taking command of the flare ship and climb to altitude— me not jumping in the crew chief's shit and ordering him to stop throwing flare fuses— me not challenging Wilk's authority. All of that will haunt me until the day I die.

The family experience was very emotional, and I said things that should I should have said years … decades earlier. But how would I have known? I had PTSD from the time I left Vietnam in 1973 and didn't realize it until 2006. That's how insidious the disease is.

How would I know that seeing decapitated soldiers, wiping brain matter and blood from my hand, carrying the dead out of the jungle, watching soldiers die would harm my psyche? How would I know that three tours filled with incoming shells, close calls, impossible circumstances, and the wounding and dying of friends would take its toll on me?

I buried it all and never had time to deal with it because there was no time, especially in combat. A soldier can't allow himself to be distracted by grieving—he has no time to cry or think about what's affecting him. He must fight, must complete the mission—must fly his ship and crew home without mental distractions.

***

After this meeting, I visited Uncle Frank and Uncle Al and Aunt Theresa. I wanted them to understand what I had been experiencing—they too were very supportive. Aunt Theresa did something that was beautiful and loving.

Aunt Theresa belonged to the Saint Theresa Society, whose members carried silk rose petals with reminders printed on them—how Saint Theresa could help someone with troubles. Aunt Theresa gave me two petals; one for "Peace" and the other for "Forgiveness."

I carry them in my wallet and look at them every day. We'll see if *forgiveness* does any good.

** PTSD **

Every painful memory you have which keeps recurring is simply your unconscious mind trying to protect you by reminding you of experiences which caused you pain and which it does not wish you to experience in the future. This is a protection mechanism which keeps you alive. Fortunately, it is possible to preserve the learnings of the memory and turn off the disturbing memory itself. When one does that, they are no longer the slave to their past memories but enjoy a mastery of their life and ability to live and respond authentically in the present.

—Roger Roger, goodreads.com

PTSD is curable when one realizes how the unconscious mind works and that the symptoms of PTSD are actually the unconscious mind attempting to protect the person experiencing them. With the right therapies it is possible to take a person with extreme PTSD and help them to neutralise all their painful memories and emotions permanently.

—Roger Roger, goodreads.com

In the military, you learn the essence of people. You see so many examples of self-sacrifice and moral courage. In the rest of life, you don't get that many opportunities to be sure of your friends.

—Adam Driver, actor and Marine Corps veteran

September 1978 to February 2009: My Thirty-One-Year War Comes to an End— PTSD, Part 15

During the last week of my first school year, I received a one-year, limited contract for the upcoming year—but with the stipulation that I must improve teacher/student relations and classroom management. An administrator informed me in a letter about *my* mindset:

> "… but he should be aware of close scrutiny next year relative to the aforementioned concerns and his future in education. Mr. Sepesy must realize that we do have skirmishes in the school business but this is not war…"

This same administrator assured everyone at a joint faculty-parent meeting during the first week of school. His message was clear, indicating student misconduct will not be tolerated … that disciplinary action would be swift and effective.

Talk about an injustice—injustice repeated day after day and then I'm to blame? I don't think so!

Okay, in retrospect and now understanding my PTSD, I realize the administrator had a point—but he misleadingly portrayed my performance, considering the environment in which I taught. I was struggling to find a balance between what *should be done* and what *was actually expected of me*—while not becoming a cog in their bureaucracy's inexcusable machine of hypocrisy.

Yes, sometimes I would wonder, *I know I'm out of the Army—but if you didn't follow rules and regulations, procedures and practices there, people got killed—and I would be held responsible and paid a price.* Interesting that I would draw such an analogy about following rules and regulations then—and three decades later, in the spring of 2006, I would come to learn that my sensitivity to injustice was a major aspect of my PTSD.

Wonderments still collided in my mind: *how could I get around the system's practice of looking the other way relevant to student discipline? How could I live with, let alone accept administrative positions that were less-than-supportive of teachers battling to maintain discipline in their classrooms?* My answers came on the last day of school while on parking lot duty.

On that day, one of the administrators surprised me by appearing in the parking lot. I approached him and struck up a conversation, including the problem of student discipline. I cited my many DRFs and the large number of incidents I had experienced involving assaults, verbal abuse, and reporting drug deals I had witnessed. "It's been a rough rookie year for me," I said. "Is this the way it usually is during a teacher's first year?"

I still remember the vivid details of that moment. The administrator grasped his hands behind his back and rocked back and forth on his heals a few times. He smiled and glanced upwards—not at me. He said and effectively ended the conversation with this comment, "Joe, you have to look the other way."

You, two-faced, double-talking, hypocrite, I thought. I wanted to hit him—right then and there; I wanted to hit him. I nodded knowingly, not in agreement—but with a sense of vindication ... and walked away.

That evening I deduced the administration would not renew my contract after next year ... and knowing I couldn't change either—not in this *bass-ackwards* environment. I would seek a teaching position elsewhere, hoping to find a system more conducive to learning, one with less bureaucratic hypocrisy.

A few weeks later, I secured a teaching position in another school system and resigned.

In September, on my new job, it became apparent that nothing relevant to student discipline had changed—nothing, and my PTSD would go unrealized for twenty-seven more years.

I looked at things from a black-and-white point of view. If management's policies said do this—I did this. If they said do that—I did that. Unknowingly, shades of gray were quite foreign to my thought processes—but for good reason—I didn't want to get into trouble for violating Board of Education policy. So, I erred on following the Board's written words. If I ignored policies, even though many others did, I feared reprimand or worse. The result was continued frustration and bewilderment, and a subsequent escalation of the ongoing problems with management—I was caught in the revolutions of a vicious circle.

One could describe my resistance as making waves—and making waves is all right— as long as one isn't merely splashing around. Did I want to make waves? No. But administrators, and fellow teachers, became displeased with my willingness to adhere to Board policies, to file grievances, and when necessary, press charges with the police. So, in the minds of so many educators, I was making waves.

So, allow me to further muddy up the waters. Consider my wave-making actions:

I refused to sign my name to documents with false information. So, my department's administrator signed her name and filed the papers.

I spoke up at meetings when administrators misrepresented or flagrantly violated our labor-management master agreement.

I filed a grievance when the administration refused to provide necessary classroom supplies. Six weeks later, I received my supplies, which augmented the programs I had written.

I challenged the administration when another teacher changed the legitimate grades I had given to students. It was the end of the year—I didn't care. That teacher was rewarded, becoming an administrator—one that later colluded with the highest level of management and tried to fire me, as I approached retirement.

I would frequently request union and legal representation at meetings with management.

The American flag had not flown on the pole in front of the building all year. Then, one morning, I asked and administrator why a flag celebrating the National Right to Read week was flapping in the breeze.

I have to give him credit—he lowered that flag and raised the Stars and Stripes.

I refused to monitor students during lunch-time movies that presented nudity and vile and profane dialogue—I would turn the projector off. Then I filed a grievance.

In response to the grievance, an upper-level administrator said, "My hands are tied. I can't do anything."

The movies continued, and I received a different duty.

I DRFed (filled out a Disciplinary Referral Form) a student-athlete for disrespectful comments during a morning study hall. His mother was president of the PTA. She raised hell—so her son suffered no consequence and could play in that afternoon's game.

Just before the study-hall period ended, an administrator entered the room and yelled at me about my poor judgment. I yelled back ... without reprisal.

I witnessed a drug dealer cruising the school's parking lot. He openly displayed his dope on the passenger's seat of his car. He threatened me.

I made a note of his car and license plate and reported that information to two administrators.

One lied about notifying the police—no one ever contacted the police. He also informed me he would do nothing, explaining, the decision was made in the best interest of the school ... and we deemed it necessary to not overreact, so you shouldn't overreact either. Besides, it's out of your hands.

It becomes understandable that maintaining employment in my new school system would become a major concern. This powerful motivator led to my union activism, which kept me fighting battle after battle. To survive, I would continue to opt for the position that best covered my ass; using management's very own, approved and established language against them. I would point to chapter and verse and say, "Well, look right here. It says blah blah ... Are you suggesting I go against Board Policy?"

Eventually administrators mellowed toward me and did tread lightly. I know most realized I wouldn't back down and would come at them with contractual or legal guns blazing. There-after, most of my major problems originated with parents and students, and from certain members of the Board and two or three administrators.

During my tenure, the administration tried to fire me five times. Because of my no-nonsense approach to classroom discipline and my involvement with the teachers' union, I became a thorn in management's side ... and their attempts to fire me, failed. In psychological jargon, I continued to nurture my sensitivity to injustice.

During that time, unknown people falsely accused me of being a racist and ineffective teacher.

Nonetheless, my confidence grew, even though by position with many teachers diminished. Some would leave the room when I entered. Some avoided me—fearing guilt by association.

***

I was a damn fine teacher and if people thought I was a hard-ass—they never saw me in action in the classroom. I was a disciplinarian, and the kids knew it. They knew I wouldn't take any crap from anyone. If they challenged me, I used the weapons at my disposal—procedures, policies, and practices. I reacted professionally and rarely displayed emotion. *Hmm, shades of PTSD.*

Did I make mistakes? Of course, I did—but admitted to them, apologized, and sought to improve myself.

During my teaching years, I taught for twelve years in high school special education classes. I wrote my own courses of instruction, which focused on survival skills, because much of the time the materials made available to me were inappropriate for teaching kids that needed to learn about everyday living situations and how to survive in the world of work. But Special Ed burned me out, so I transferred to the junior high level where I taught Social Studies and a few English courses.

When that bell rang—it was showtime! I was prepared and presented a thorough and appropriate lesson. While meeting the objectives at hand, my lessons were also effective and entertaining. My classroom offered a pleasant atmosphere—one conducive to learning. I decorated it with maps and pictures, daily and weekly agenda, and inspirational words that were applied whenever necessary to make a point. I balanced class time, allotting for presentation and discussion, sometimes enhanced by audio-visual aids, and time for seat work.

If the students didn't give a damn, if their parents didn't give a damn—nothing I tried really mattered. That was the reality, a reality too often blurred or covered up by people in the profession.

***

PTSD influenced me throughout my teaching career. I had problems with management—or in PTSD terminology—problems with authority figures. *Hmm, the Chickenman Captain that damn near led a suicide mission comes to mind. Captain Botch wanted to fly through the kill zone. That out-of-touch Major Farcic said, "If you receive fire—it will be friendly fire. So do not return fire."*

During my union's most conflicted times, I served as a strike leader and held several positions of leadership—just like flying Yellow 1. I ran meetings succinctly, similar to giving radio briefings—say what must be said, then shut up; I conducted my agenda and procedures similar to leading a flight of eight Masher Hueys on combat assaults—no bullshit, present the material, answer questions—get the job done.

Because of rigid military training, followed by three combat tours with over two-thousand combat flight hours, my PTSD manifested itself as a continuation of that training, my experiences and performance. I was accustomed to choosing between; kill or be killed, live or die, and the ramifications of potentially deadly decision-making processes—while being expected to complete my missions.

Comparatively, in civilian life, I found that such notions of right versus wrong seemed to be diminished or vague—right was right sometimes, and wrong was wrong ... *depending.*

But how does one justify one's rationales and actions when hypocrisy continues to be the flavor of the day? My wonderments persisted: *How could I ignore the flagrant demonstrations of inept practices and live with myself? I had to press on— and did!*

Sometimes a foxhole mentality helps a combat veteran get through a tough situation. During my years of teaching, that philosophy involved telling myself that things could be worse; reminding myself of ways to improve my odds of survival; determining which battles to choose and what tactics to employ and to what extent; knowing I have and could fight the good fight, not physically, but with other weapons including knowledge of policies and procedures—more so than management; listening more than speaking—then hanging management with their own words; documenting events and relying on support personnel. I should mention that a small group of like-minded teachers and union officials came to my aid, and we had each other's backs.

My PTSD became a double-edged sword on the quasi-positive side, by prompting my foxhole mentality to surface and employed, thus using a by-the-book approach to classroom management and contract enforcement and conducting business.

On the negative side, I experienced stress, anger and depression and would become distant or numb, irritable and frustrated. I challenged and battled management, trusted very few, and confrontations were many. I was hypervigilant, and I led the charge for the union of teachers that I represented—all took their toll mentally and a few times, physically.

***

Using a foxhole mentality during my years of teaching should be understandable. In a sense I was still at war, not with helicopters and machine guns over jungles and rice paddies, but in run-down buildings of a dying urban environment where many didn't seem to care, didn't want to care; where many denied how bad things really were.

The fighting continued, even with PTSD counseling, through my final few years of teaching. However, during that time, I began understanding shades of gray, seeing the differences between compromise and looking-the-other-way, and I mellowed with my approach to management during disputes about Board policies and my union's collective bargaining agreement.

***

Thirty-one years is a long time. I was living ... no; I was existing in an environment permeated with hypocrisy and incompetence—a place where logic and common sense seemed to be foreign concepts. Consider the administrator's "look the other way" comment as both my vindication and condemnation of their broken system.

Yes, thirty-one years is a long time, made to feel even longer when filled with anxiety and fear, anger and hatred, disappointment and depression, lies and distortions, vindictiveness and hostility, not knowing and loneliness, self-doubt and second-guessing, high blood pressure and sleepless nights, and the awful truth that I was right but still to blame, and to an extent, because I didn't know that I was suffering from PTSD.

As previewed earlier in this memoir, I was also forced to retire from teaching in February 2009. But that was a victory since the Board wanted to fire me in the spring of 2006, before I would have thirty-five years of service, an enormous factor in determining my retirement pension. My lawyer and the Board's lawyer worked out a deal that was less than appealing but would save me much distress.

My assignment from September 2006 through February 2009 involved non-classroom assignments. So, in the Board's office building, I worked in an air-conditioned office with no students and no one really overseeing me. I didn't take advantage of the arrangement—but; it was nice being my own boss.

Unfortunately, I did not complete one substantial assignment by the day of my retirement. So, I turned in what had been completed and the rest in rough-note form. I told my the administrator that I would work one more year and was open to negotiations concerning compensation. The administrator never got back to me and my retirement appeared as a terse sentence or two in Board minutes—nothing else. My thirty-one-year war of teaching was over—I had survived, just like my previous war—I had survived.

One of the happiest moments of my life occurred when I pulled out of the Board's parking lot and saw its building for the last time in my rear-view mirror.

Done! They didn't get me!

Sure, military combat is scary... but in some ways combat seems a little easier than personal relationships. At least in combat, the enemy is honest enough to claim themselves as such.

—Steve Maraboli, goodreads.com

2009: Private Matters—PTSD, Part 16

My wife and I divorced in April 2009. I have chosen not to elaborate on the problems that were experienced during twenty-five years of marriage, but I must mention its end. Without doubt, one of the contributing factors to the demise of our marriage was PTSD—to what extent is a matter of opinion.

***

I now know that my life's two biggest mistakes were becoming a teacher and getting married. I was not emotionally equipped for either. But I toughed out my teaching career because life got in the way—marriage and family, mortgage and financial responsibilities.

I suspected early on that my marriage was a mistake, but I thought things would get better. Not until I discovered PTSD and viewed myself objectively and from an informed point of view, did I come to these realizations. Now I know, PTSD and in particular, suppressing emotions and applying a foxhole mentality was not the best mix for either endeavor.

"General Norman Schwarzkopf spoke of Vietnam, 'The outcome of the Vietnam War was political defeat, but it was not a military defeat.'"

—B.G. Burkett, *Stolen Valor*, Verity Press, Page 49, 1998

"NVA leaders who fought against LTC Hal Moore's Skytroopers of the 1st Cav were astounded by the 'fanaticism' displayed by the American soldiers."

—B. G. Burkett, *Stolen Valor*, Verity Press, Page 62, 1998

To us you seemed beyond brave and fearless ... that you would come to us in the middle of battle in those flimsy thin-skinned crates ... and in the storm of fire you would sit there behind that Plexiglas seeming so patient and so calm and so vulnerable ... waiting for the off-loading and the on-loading. We thought you were God's own lunatics ... and we loved you ... still do.

—From Joe Galloway's speech, "God's Own Lunatics," about helicopter pilots, 2 July 2000, during the Vietnam Helicopter Pilots Association reunion

7 and 8 March 2009: Louisville, Kentucky

I drove to Louisville, Kentucky this morning to attend one day of the Ohio River LZ Chapter's (VHPA) reunion. This was my first time attending a regional function of the VHPA. If I had arrived the previous night, I could have logged a few minutes of stick time in a Huey—for free—a generous gesture offered by one of the Chapter's members.

The emcee at the dinner welcomed approximately 230 guests, including the speakers for the evening; Lieutenant General Hal Moore and war correspondent Joe Galloway, veterans of the battle at LZ X-Ray, in November 1965.

General Moore spoke briefly, expressing an infantryman's love for helicopter pilots. Joe Galloway took the mic next, and he too embraced helicopter pilots for their undaunted support of American infantrymen who counted on them to deliver supplies, medevac the wounded and dead, and provide close air-support gun cover.

One of Joe's comments spoke volumes, "We hated you when you dropped us off ... but loved you when you came for us."

Hearing words like that was very special and brought a lump to my throat.

After the formalities, General Moore and Joe Galloway signed their two books about the Battle of LZ X-Ray. I had the honor of meeting both men who signed my copies of *We Were Soldiers Once...and Young* and *We Are Soldiers Still* and my Joe Kline print, "God's Own Lunatics."

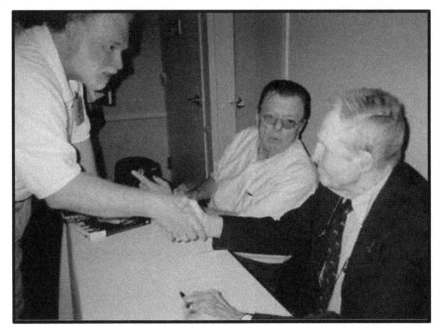

The author meeting Joe Galloway and General Hal Moore (Author's private collection).

General Hal Moore signing the author's copy of the Joe Kline print, "God's Own Lunatics." Please refer to the chapter "10 August 1970: LRRP Extraction" in Once We Flew, Volume I, for my introduction to the story of "God's Own Lunatics." (Author's private collection).

***

Lieutenant General Harold "Hal" Moore was born in Bardstown, Kentucky on 13 February 1922 and died on 10 February 2017 at the age of 95. He was the recipient of the US Army's second highest award, the Distinguished Service Cross, for his actions at the Battle of LZ X-Ray, in Vietnam in November of 1965. Rest in peace, General Moore. GARRY OWEN!

"The fact that ... helicopters are eagerly sought in large numbers by air forces, armies and navies all over the world serves to underscore their value.

—Bill Gunston, Mike Spick, *Modern Fighting Helicopters,* 1998

11 June 2009: Crazy Horse, Masher Huey 545

July 2008

I read the inquiry in the July 2008 edition of the 1st Cavalry's newspaper. Sergeant John Stokes of the Greenville, South Carolina Sheriff's Department requested information about an aircraft that had been assigned to Bravo 227, aircraft 69-15545. I immediately recalled 545 as Crazy Horse, Major Fisher's bird when he was the CO— of course, I had to contact John Stokes.

John told me about 545's latest journeys. Aircraft 545 had come to his department via a National Guard unit without charge and with the stipulation that the bird's use would be for official county operations. John was the EMT for the Sheriff's air rescue unit, so 545 was made-to-order for his law enforcement agency. They spruced up 545 and modified her for air-rescue.

John invited me to South Carolina, and I accepted. I contacted Randy Clark, and we both decided that we should check out the former Masher Huey in the future.

11 June 2009

I drove to Randy's home in Greensboro, North Carolina, on 10 June 2008. The next morning, he and I drove to the Greenville to meet John Stokes. After introductions, John informed us that the department's pilot, Chris Hine, had called off sick. That disappointed us and dashed any chance of flying the bird. The other disappointment was 545 would remain in the hangar so we could not fully appreciate her presence.

After getting acquainted, the three of us climbed around 545, reminisced, and took pictures.

John told us that the guys in his department were not only interested in the history of 545's service in the Cav, but also Bravo 227 personnel and Phuoc Vinh. Unfortunately, I could not provide any information about the damage incurred by 545 during her last flight, which occurred in II Corps in April 1971, when I was home on leave. However, Randy and I could address John's other areas of interest.

We thanked John for taking the time on his day off to reunite us with 545 and we departed, somewhat disappointed but thankful that we had revisited 545. We did not know that we would see 545 again with someone very special.

"Anchors Aweigh, my boys, Anchors Aweigh!
Farewell to foreign Shores, we sail at break of day-ay-ay-ay;
Through our last night ashore, drink to the foam,
Until we meet once more, here's wishing you a happy voyage home!"

—"Anchors Aweigh"[1]

15 June 2009: Uncle Frank Died Today— PTSD, Part 17

After a six-week illness another of the Greatest Generation and my Godfather, Uncle Frank Sepesy, died today at eighty-four. Uncle Frank, the second son of Sandor and Anna Sepesy, was buried in his US Navy uniform—the same uniform he wore during World War II.

On 19 March 1945, approximately fifty miles from the mainland of Japan, Uncle Frank was serving on the aircraft carrier, the USS *Benjamin Franklin*. Attacked by two Japanese dive bombers that delivered two 550-pound bombs, the ship was soon ablaze. Uncle Frank became trapped below deck in a midship galley that was jammed with three hundred sailors.

Lieutenant JG Donald A. Gary discovered them and led them to safety through smoke-filled passageways and metal duct works that led to a narrow walkway along the ship's hull, forty feet above the waterline.

---

[1]—"Anchors Aweigh," revised lyrics by MCPON John Hagan, USN (Ret), 1997

After negotiating the treacherous walkway, Uncle Frank climbed up to the deck and joined the fire-fighting and evacuation of wounded onto the destroyer Santa Fe.

Uncle Frank's hands became too raw from handling ropes, so he moved to a line of sailors that were passing live shells, as with a bucket brigade, then heaved over the side. Uncle Frank could use his forearms to hold the shells.

After the battle, Uncle Frank found himself on the Santa Fe which sailed to Pearl Harbor.

The "Big Ben" sustained major damage, thus earning the nickname "The ship that wouldn't die." The ship's crew of twenty-six hundred sailors and officers sustained heavy losses: 807 KIAs and 487 WIAs.

The US Navy fully restored the *Franklin* but never returned her to sea duty, decommissioning her in 1964.

LJG Gary was awarded the Medal of Honor for his heroic action during the attack on the *Ben Franklin*.

After the war, Uncle Frank returned to Youngstown, Ohio. He served his country again during the Korean War before settling down in Struthers, Ohio.

** PTSD **

The following excerpt from my brief eulogy for Uncle Frank which contains a comment about PTSD and its effects on me.

The world is a better place .... for Frank that rings more true than any bell of any cathedral's tower, anywhere on God's Earth. I speak the truth and the indisputable proof is here, before us, on the faces and in the hearts of you good people ... you, who have gathered here, know this to be true....

Frank had touched us as a machinist, bus driver, chef, singer ... whatever the role he assumed for so many ... a man whose presence had indeed made the world a better place.

I have one such memory, from Monday, the day Uncle Frank, my Godfather died. You see, even in death, Frank's magic continued—he touched my life again, but more profoundly than ever before. I've had trouble with emotions ... understanding and expressing them ... and living with them. Thirty minutes after Uncle Frank's death and hearing the news, I broke down and cried like a baby. For only the second time in nearly four decades, I felt ... I freely released genuine emotion from a heart long troubled and unable to do so. Thank you. Uncle Frank, thank you for helping me to feel again ... to both grieve and celebrate ... to heal.

2009: It Still Hurts—PTSD, Part 18

Concerning PTSD, I've been told, "Why don't you just get over it?"

I never knew how to respond to such an unfair question—but now I do, thanks to nearly three years of group therapy and four years of one-on-one therapy. Now, if I'm ever asked that question, I consider it rhetorical and don't respond—but that doesn't really satisfy me either. But there are answers, as described so beautifully and eloquently below. So, if I can reach into the recesses of my memory and recall those words and their meanings, I can explain my feelings and provide answers.

> "He knew that this was because the soldier was still in him, and that it would be in him for a long time, for soldiers who have been bloodied are soldiers forever. Even when they finally settle down, the settling is tenuous for when they close their eyes, they see their comrades who have fallen.
>
> They cannot forget, that they do not forget, that they never allow themselves to heal completely, is their way of expressing their love for friends who have perished."

—Mark Helprin, *A Soldier of the Great War,* Mariner Books, 2005

The combat veteran is different from other veterans. The reason is mentioned above, "... for soldiers who have been bloodied are soldiers forever." Consider that with the following observations.

186

We have shared the incommunicable experience of war. We have felt ... we still feel the passion of life at its top. In our youths, our hearts were touched with fire.

—Supreme Court Justice Oliver Wendell Holmes (Six-time-wounded, Civil War veteran.)

"Holmes was struggling with himself to put into words what every soldier who has faced combat knows in his or her guts. That paradoxically, when your life is most threatened, when violent death is possible at any moment—everything is vivified, the intensity of experience heightened to a level not felt in ordinary life.

War creates a terror, an excruciating unbearable terror that is not only repellant but undeniably and inexplicably compelling. It is an almost indescribable feeling that survivors of war from the beginning of recorded history have found overwhelming, intimidating, and haunting, yet also seductive and spellbinding."

—Geoffrey C. Ward and Ken Burns, *The War, An Intimate History 1941–1945,* Knoph, November 2010

***

The above passages are reinforced by this memoir's entry, "1994: Cronkite Was Wrong, Schwarzkopf Was Right!" in particular the words of CBS reporter Eric Sevareid.

** PTSD **

Healing is not an overnight process: it is a daily cleansing of pain, it is a daily healing of your life.

—Leon Brown, azquotes.com

"Today, more than 23 million veterans walk among us. Nearly 3 million receive disability compensation, and many more owe their lives to an anonymous corpsman or medic. Millions of Americans and their families are profoundly grateful."

—Scott McGaugh, *Battlefield Angels: Saving Lives from Valley Forge to Afghanistan,* Osprey Publishing, 2011

1 to 4 July 2009: VHPA Reunion, Philadelphia—Band of Brothers, Part 8

I was looking forward to my second VHPA reunion. Upon arrival, it was most enjoyable to meet with the Mashers from previous generations that I had met in Washington DC. Since Lou Bartolotta lived one or two miles away in Old Philadelphia, he came and went throughout the reunion.

Tricky Dick arrived for one day, then returned to Allentown, Pennsylvania. Randy's fellow-pilot from US Air, Terry Glendy, from Florida; and Choo Choo Coleman from Oregon were there for the duration.

Of course, we told stories and talked about our tours of duty. One story that was shared by Lou stands out in my mind. "I'll never forget my drill sergeant's first words to us," began Lou. "There we were, standing at attention and he says, 'You will clean yo' assholes! I will not have dirty assholes in my barracks.'"

I always wondered how the drill sergeant would know the cleanliness of his platoon's assholes—maybe better to not know.

On the second day, I attended the formal dinner and sat with Dave Greene, a Bravo Good Dealer who served before my time in Nam. The emcee called for order and immediately introduced the "New York City Emerald Society Bagpipe Band."

Drums pounded and pipes wailed from the adjoining hall as the band entered the ballroom playing "Garry Owen!" They played "Garry Owen," the Cav's song!

Covered with goose bumps, I stood, clapped and cheered with the other guests. It was magnificent!

The band stood in formation at the front of the room and played "God Bless America" followed by the five service songs. Then the band played "The Star-Spangled Banner," as a local singer sang our national anthem—the correct way without personalized yelping, moaning and screaming, and the altering of the melody.

The pipers and drummers commanded our attention from their first beat through the last beat of their exit. They stood at attention and marched stone-faced, with intensity and pride. We clapped and shouted again as they exited. We felt so proud, and it was mutual—they felt our pride.

All Mashers; Jim "Choo Choo" Coleman, Lou Bartolotta, the author, Randy Clark, Dave Greene, Terry Glendy (Author's private collection).

Just before the meal, a somber toast to the missing man brought balance to the event after its rousing beginning. That brought tears to many eyes. I admit I struggled for a while—then lost it. Dave put his arms around me and embraced me—a band-of-brothers moment—yes, *my* band of brothers.

After the meal and an hour of dancing, I changed clothes and met with the Mashers outside for an impromptu street party. At midnight, the cop on duty threatened to arrest all of us unless we sang happy birthday to America—which we did loudly.

***

During this reunion, I met Brigadier General John C. "Doc" Bahnsen, author of an excellent book, *American Warrior: A Combat Memoir of Vietnam*. Our conversation eventually moved to awards and decorations. In a nutshell, General Bahnsen thought I deserved a Purple Heart from the day of my shoot-down, and a Distinguished Flying Cross for my action with WO1 Jim Rose, on 14 June 1970, the emergency resupply at LZ Ready. The general was confident that with his contacts at the Pentagon, my Air Medal with V Device would be upgraded to a DFC. He also thought that receiving the Purple Heart would be difficult.

After months of telephone conversations, letters and documenting, the Army denied both requests. I must add, after reading the general's book, followed by his tireless efforts to help me, he is a man of his word, and still deeply cares about the men he served with during our war.

Thank you, General Bahnsen.

** PTSD **

"Triggers can happen when you least expect them. When you think all the emotional wounds are healed something can happen that reminds you there is still a scar."

—Alexandra Eva May, unclutteryourmind.com, "90+ PTSD Quotes to Help Survivors Cope with Trauma," by Rachel Sharpe

"Regard your soldiers as your children, and they will follow you into the deepest valleys; look upon them as your own beloved sons, and they will stand by you even unto death."

—Sun Tzu, *Art of War*

15 July and 30 September 2009: Reunited with Mr. Clean—Band of Brothers, Part 9

While at the VHPA reunion in Philadelphia, the conversation eventually turned to Major Harold Fisher, affectionately known to us as Mr. Clean. No one had heard a word from or about our former commanding officer since we left his command nearly forty years ago. Somehow, I received the assignment of tracking the elusive officer and hopefully establishing contact with him.

Randy knew I was a member of the 1st Cavalry Association and he recommended I start there. *Why didn't I think of that?*

When I got home, I contacted the Cav Association and sure enough; they had information on Major Fisher—he lived in the Rockwell, North Carolina area. I dialed information, and lo-and-behold, there was a listing for Harold R. Fisher in Rockwell.

I dialed the number, and a woman answered—Major Fisher's wife—success!

Mrs. Clean informed me I had just missed her husband, who had left for Kansas to attend another reunion with soldiers from his first tour. She assured me she would take my name and number and that Mr. Clean would call me upon his return.

I called Randy and gave him the good news, which astounded him. But hearing that Mr. Clean lived in Rockwell, North Carolina, about an hour's drive from Randy, who lived in Greensboro, North Carolina, astounded him more so.

***

15 July 2009

Ten days passed quickly. Then, the telephone rang, "Ah, hello," said a bass Southern voice, "is this Joey Sepesy?"

"Mr. Clean? Is that you?"

"Well, yes, it is," was the answer in that deliberate southern accent, the unmistakable voice of Major Harold R. Fisher.

"I'll be damned. We've been looking for you, wondering about you for years! I don't believe I'm actually talking to you."

"Well, you'd better believe it because it's me."

I calmed down and settled into a normal conversation with Mr. Clean. After catching up on each other's life, I asked him if he would be interested in seeing Crazy Horse again. "You can't be serious!"

"Yes, I am, Sir, in fact, your old bird, 545, is within an hour's travel time of your house."

I know Mr. Clean was struggling with disbelief. So, I told him about the extraordinary chain of events; from reading the article about 545 to locating him. I asked Mr. Clean if he would like to visit 545 and maybe take her for a flight.

"Oh, this is too good—you mean to tell me you can arrange that?"

"Nothing's guaranteed. But I know the sheriff's department in Greenville County, South Carolina would welcome you with the red-carpet treatment. They're really into the history of their bird, Vietnam, and the guys that flew helicopters."

Mr. Clean agreed to visit 545, with Randy taking over and working out the details since he had kept in contact with the Greenville Sheriff's department. I wrapped up the conversation, said goodbye and called Randy. After briefing him, he immediately called Mr. Clean to plan our long-awaited reunion.

29 September 2009

I drove to Randy's home in Greensboro, North Carolina today. He had made all the arrangements with John Stokes, the EMT with the Greenville Sheriff's Department and their pilot, Chris Hine. It also excited me to learn that another Bravo Good Dealer, Captain Richard Cross, "Tricky Dick", would arrive later in the day from Pennsylvania.

30 September 2009

Major Harold Fisher seated in 545, thirty-nine years after flying her in Vietnam, Randy Clark, the author, and Richard Cross pose with their commanding officer. (Author's private collection).

Randy, Trick, and I departed Greensboro early in the morning to rendezvous with Major Fisher at a Cracker Barrel restaurant near his home. During our ride I told Randy and Trick what I remembered about Crazy Horse, UH-1, 545.

Crazy Horse migrated to II Corps in April 1971, after Randy and I DEROSed. While I was on leave, prior to returning to Bravo 227, the Mashers were running combat assaults all over the Central Highlands and the coastal regions. During one of those missions, 545 was damaged by enemy fire and shipped back to the US for repairs. The Army refitted her and returned her to duty with a National Guard unit. Nearly four decades later, the Guard would retire 545 and give her to the Greenville, South Carolina Sheriff's Department.

Randy parked his jeep in the Cracker Barrel's parking lot. In a few minutes Mr. Clean would arrive. Trick and Randy went inside for a minute while I waited on the porch, sitting in one of the restaurant's rocking chairs. Within seconds, a red pickup truck pulled in and parked. The form of a man I had known so very well emerged. He locked his vehicle and strode onto the wooden porch. I stood and walked toward him. Our gazes met, and we smiled. I don't recall what we said, but we grabbed each other and embraced. It was a wonderful and emotional moment.

As we walked to the entrance, Randy and Trick emerged through the doorway. Again, more smiles and hugs—what a beautiful reunion.

We ate breakfast and got caught up on our lives, being perfectly comfortable with one another throughout—that band-of-brother's thing was most clear.

After breakfast we piled into Randy's jeep and headed for Greenville. We talked about Vietnam, other Good Dealers, missions, and of course, 545. I also told Trick and Mr. Clean about my reunion with 048 at Mott's Military Museum.

Within the hour we were pulling into the Greenville County airport where Chris Hine, John Stokes, and other members of the rescue unit greeted us. Major Fisher was eager to see 545—he kept edging around the hangar, trying to glimpse his old bird. So, all of us walked across the tarmac.

A group of about twelve other people were milling about near 545—other members of the Sheriff's Department and one videographer from a local television station.

We had warned Mr. Clean that Crazy Horse wore a new dress, dark blue with white trim and the Sheriff's Department markings. But that didn't matter. As Mr. Clean approached his old aircraft, he stopped short and swallowed hard as emotions stirred inside. I put my arm around his shoulder and said, "There she is, Sir. Go say hello." Knowing what he was experiencing, I stepped aside so he could be alone.

Mr. Clean stepped forward as tears welled in his eyes. He stood by 545's nose, reached out, and tenderly touched her. "My, my, my, all those years ago, we were together.

Chris Hine opened the AC's door and Major Fisher climbed into the left seat, the same seat he had occupied thirty-nine years earlier in Vietnam—where he now reminisced.

After posing for dozens of pictures, answering endless questions, and the telling of war stories, Major Fisher was interviewed by a local television videographer in which he described some of his war experiences with the aviators and 545 of Bravo 227. He stressed how durable and reliable the Huey was—how it brought hundreds of men home, mission after mission and day after day. He was quite eloquent, and he explained what it was like holding rein on a bunch of teenage warrant officers and slightly older commissioned officers—how to keep their love-of-flying in check while still completing their missions … and getting home alive.

Major Fisher commanded Bravo 227 from August 1970, to February 1971, his second combat tour of duty in Vietnam. Flying out of Phuoc Vinh, he led his young aviators, flying their Hueys on combat assaults, and direct combat support missions for units of the 1st Air Cav and ARVN (Army of the Republic of Vietnam) units. He accumulated 900 combat hours while with Bravo 227, most of which were logged with 545.

The Greenville Sheriff arrived during the next few minutes.

Randy had prepared two plaques, each with a picture of 545 in her earlier days as Crazy Horse. He presented one to Mr. Clean and the other to Chris Hine. We adjourned for lunch and then returned to the airfield. All the dignitaries and guests had gone, and we suspected something was up. Unbeknownst to us, the Sheriff instructed Chris Hine to take Mr. Clean for a flight.

That news thrilled and disappointed Randy, Trick, and I: thrilled for Mr. Clean, but disappointed that we wouldn't fly, not even permitted to sit in the cargo deck while he flew. But this was Mr. Clean's moment, his day with his Crazy Horse— to love her one more time.

So, from the sidelines the three of us grounded aviators watched Mr. Clean crank up 545 and away they flew, one traffic pattern and a bit of hovering. Major

Fisher smiled that all-too-familiar smile we had seen so many times before—he loved it!

We thanked Chris and John for a memorable day. During our drive, the four of us talked about our days as Bravo Good Dealers. We asked questions and offered answers and clarifications when memories cooperated. At the Cracker Barrel, we four Mashers made our goodbyes with the promise to gather again soon, with other Mashers.

The best CO a soldier could want; Major Harold "Mr. Clean" Fisher, at 75, reunited with his UH-1H, Crazy Horse, in 2009 Author's private collection).

PTSD doesn't make you weak. It makes you a survivor.

—DaShanne Stokes, goodreads.com

Let us read, and let us dance; these two amusements will never do any harm to the world.

—Voltaire, 1785

November 2009: Talk the Talk, Walk the Walk ... Dance the Dance—PTSD, Part 19

In the summer of the 2009 I encountered a friend, another teacher from my school system. Steve was dancing at a local establishment and moved beautifully across the floor—having had lessons was obvious. I asked him about his involvement with ballroom dancing and who he would recommend for lessons. He gave me the name and number of a dance instructor, "Give her a call. She's the best."

When I got home, I placed Steve's note on the refrigerator under a magnet—and there it stayed for five months, until just before Thanksgiving.

***

In November 2009, discussion in my severe PTSD group began with, "You can talk the talk—now, can you walk the walk?"

Doctor Echols asked all of us to write three goals that would show that we had grown and gained an understanding of our PTSD: that we could employ the coping skills we had learned, and that we could move beyond discussion and truly, "walk the walk."

I was the last to speak as Dr. Echols went around the room. "Joe, what are your three goals?"

197

"I want to finish my Vietnam memoir. It's been in the works for a long time and I haven't been spending time on it like I should be doing."

"Tell us about the memoir," said Dr. Echols.

I told everyone about how I had documented the World War II military service of my Dad, and Uncles and how they suggested I write about my military service.

"I see," said Dr. Echols, "and your other two goals?"

"Well, I'd like to get my guitar out of the closet and see if I can still play. It's been years since I played it, and I'd really like to see if I remembered anything."

"Oh, you play the guitar," said Dr. Echols.

"Yeah, started when I was five years old—but haven't played professionally or anything worthy of note since about 1977."

"Okay, and your third goal?" asked Dr. Echols.

"Well, I don't know how this one is going to go over, but I love music, all kinds—so, for the past few months I've been thinking about taking up ballroom dancing."

Smiles appeared on every guy in the room, followed by chuckles and comments. Dr. Echols also smiled and said, "Oo, ballroom dancing—that's nice!"

"Thanks, Doc, I've been interested in dancing for some time now, but haven't had the motivation. I think I'll give it a shot."

The good-natured kidding continued for a bit. Then Dr. Mako told us we would have our last session in three weeks, and that we would all have to report about how we walked our walk during that time.

When I got home, I booked my first private dance lesson with dance instructor Lynda Styles.

After three weeks, the members of my severe PTSD group assembled at a restaurant near the VA clinic. After our breakfast, Dr. Echols reminded us of our last meeting and the goals each of us had set for ourselves. Again, I would be the last to speak.

"Well, I started writing my memoir again, and once I got it going, I really stayed on it." I continued with, "I got my guitar out and was right—remembered little, and my fingers stumbled all over the frets. It was a frustrating."

"So, what do you plan on doing about playing the guitar?"

"I'll practice some finger dexterity exercises and chords, maybe take a few lessons and get the calluses back on my fingers. But I don't know how far I'll go."

"And your third goal?" asked Dr. Echols, recalling with a smile it was about ballroom dancing.

"Three weeks ago, I had my first ballroom dancing lesson—and I loved it. I was hooked after ten minutes! Have a wonderful teacher and I've already been out social dancing three times."

"Oo," cooed Dr. Echols. "Tell us, what are you dancing?"

"I started with swing, rumba and the tango."

I explained how easily the basic steps of swing and rumba came to me and how I was already enjoying music I had never heard before.

"But, the tango—well, that might take some time. There's a lot going on with posture." I raised my arms up as if in closed dance position. "Holding the proper frame—lots of stuff."

The guys responded in an amused and joking fashion, but this time showed more interest in my musical endeavor. "What about the women?" asked one member of the group.

"I want you guys to know, holding a woman close to you while sensual music is playing—that's really something—especially when dancing the rumba and tango."

That was my last meeting with the intensive PTSD group. I continued one-on-one counseling sessions with Dr. Mako. My progress pleased him and he was adamant about how dancing had helped me cope with my PTSD in several ways, including socialization, concentration on a new interest, and trusting in an authority figure—my teacher.

Both Dr. Echols and Dr. Mako have retired. Since then, I have continued meeting with new counselors.

Dance instructor, Lynda Styles, and the author, September 2010, after performing their tango routine to the music, "Blue Tango" (Author's private collection).

My beautiful teacher, Lynda Styles, is incredibly talented—the best possible teacher. I have shared the stories about my shoot-down and injury, and the subsequent operations with Lynda and new dancing friends. Their encouragement and understanding—their friendships are priceless.

Linda considers me an ongoing challenge because of my physical limitations, especially balance, and my determination, which sometimes interferes with her syllabus, technique and approach. She has to remind me she's the boss and reins me in occasionally to work on basic steps, checking my enthusiasm and creativity, insisting I maintain a strong dance foundation.

Dancing has been a transformational element in my life. I have lost thirty-five pounds, gained confidence, and met dozens of fabulous and talented people. I'm never at a loss for companionship and entertainment, and now the enjoyment of a variety of the most beautiful music from many genres.

From late 2009 to the present, I became proficient in thirteen genres of dance. However, I can now only safely dance eight. In 2016, my advancing nerve damage caused one-hundred percent drop-foot with my left foot and about seventy-five percent with the right foot. As a result, I wear leg braces, supplied by the Department of Veterans Affairs. The VA has also provided for physical therapy with competent experts.

My problems with balance and pain persist, but Lynda is forever vigilant and thoughtful, and has circumvented my shortcomings by adjusting techniques and employing specific exercises. Lynda Styles has changed my life and I am thankful for meeting her. I consider her a dear friend and confidante.

I still walk with a limp, and use a cane for stability and safety, however, when I dance there is no limp—actually, I dance better than I walk. I have performed in front of hundreds of people, helped Lynda as her assistant during group lessons, and helped at her studio, A Time to Dance.

You've been so used to fighting Wars with a gun in your hand that you forget to put it down. Not every fight requires a weapon of some kind, and not everything is a fight.

—Lori Llewellyn, quoteslyfe.com

Autumn 2000 through Spring 2010: Parking Lot Man—PTSD, Part 20

In 2000, I got a part-time job at a university, with its parking services department—and wouldn't you know it—same old shit, just like teaching—trouble with management.

Management told me to write tickets—I wrote tickets. They told me to not let people park here or there—I didn't let people park here or there. They told me to report suspicious people to the police—I did so.

I took my job seriously and brought in over $33,000 worth of fines to the university. Drivers disputed many of those tickets, part of the policy established by the department—maybe too many guilty individuals disputed their tickets. They just didn't want to pay and would say anything not to pay and to make me look like the bad guy.

On Saturdays, during football season, I was in charge of a VIP lot. People that parked there needed special permits. No permit—no park—simple. But one afternoon, a state politician drove in and parked in my VIP lot.

I approached him and nicely told him that without the proper permit, he could not park his car here.

"Do you know who I am?" he asked.

"No."

The politician continued, insisting that he would park in my lot.

So, I continued to tell him, "No, Sir," eventually adding, "If you don't move your car, I'll have it towed."

This important person then lectured me about how I should accommodate him, ending with, "This isn't the end of this!" Then after wasting another minute, he backed out of my lot and went somewhere else.

This scenario repeated itself several times with other important people or people who thought they were important, therefore meriting special treatment. I'm sure management received phone calls about their interactions with me.

Over the course of my ten years at the university I had occasion to contact the police because of suspicious activities on campus in particular, in its many parking lots. Ticketers like me were told to do so while patrolling the lots. I did so on more than a few occasions—usually when the suspicious individuals appeared to be pushing drugs.

I was told by one police officer that most of the cops didn't appreciate my calls of suspicion. That made sense because of the looks of consternation on some officers' faces upon arriving at the suspicious locations, accompanied by unreceptive attitudes and remarks.

"Hey, just doing what I was told to do," would be my usual comeback.

And then there were the professors and administrators who interacted with me.

One uppity and important professor with political connections bitched up a storm after I ticketed her car three or four times for the same infractions: parking without a permit, and parking in an area not designated for parking. So, management told me to avoid the place where this important person continued to park her important car.

I ticketed the university president for parking in a fire zone next to a high-rise dorm—it was ignored.

I ticketed one of the upper-level administrators for parking on the university's core, a series of sidewalks, surrounded by buildings at the center of the campus. That level of offense dictated that I contact the police immediately—so I did.

The officer arrived and confirmed the procedure that I was following. As I was placing the ticket on the car's window, the car's owner arrived—he was pissed. I explained the offense to him, but the administrator didn't care.

"I was meeting with the president and you don't keep him waiting!"

I pointed to a lot only fifty yards away. "You could have parked there, thus avoiding this predicament."

"I've heard about you," he said in a menacing way with a wagging finger.

I turned away, thanked the officer for his help and departed the scene.

Minutes later, management called me on the radio and told to report to the operations base. I was asked to explain the incident. Management said not to worry about it and sent me back to make my rounds.

In my mind, the incident was closed. But wouldn't you know it? The same offense and same driver occurred a few weeks later. *Damn it!* I thought, *I don't need this shit!* But I wrote a ticket, called the police and went on my way—this time without another display of ignorance and arrogance from the administrator.

True to form, management called me on the radio minutes later and told to report to operations base. This time, an administrator delivered a message from the top. I was told me to go home and think about what had occurred.

"We'll give you a call," he said.

Well, I received one call months later—they were hurting for extra help—but never again after that. So, I made it official a few months later and resigned—I'm sure, much to the pleasure of the a few administrators.

Now, I may have been rocking the boat, but I wasn't just splashing away either. I was not looking the other way, and I was following the written policies as instructed by supervisory personnel. My actions were correct, and I addressed glaring violations as I would for any other routine violation.

I also wondered about management testing ticketers—watching to see if obvious infractions were being addressed—that we were doing our jobs appropriately. Other ticketers also thought that might be the case.

After each football game, firework displays filled the sky. Thumps that sounded just like the firing of in-coming mortar shells, were the prelude to each overhead explosion. The first couple of times the fireworks began, my body would spasm, and with no thought, I would cover my head and crouch down. After realizing the noise had nothing to do with in-coming rockets or mortars, I would calm down after a minute. But clearing my head of the subsequent intrusive thoughts and memories wasn't so easy.

After a couple of games, I would prepare myself for the sounds of the pyrotechnic displays; the thumps and the explosions. I still got anxious and breathed a sigh of relief after the demonstrations.

Loud noises and sudden noises, regardless of volume, continue to affect me. For years, before beginning counseling, my entire body would jerk and spasm, and I would cover my head and crouch down for cover.

** PTSD **

"What Is PTSD Hypervigilance?"

"One of the many hyper-arousal symptoms of Post-Traumatic Stress Disorder is hyper vigilance, and this refers to the experience of being constantly tense and 'on guard'- your brain is on high alert in order to be certain danger is not near....

People displaying hypervigilance can be so involved in their scrutiny of what's around them, that they tend to ignore their family and friends. Often, they will overreact to loud sounds and bangs, unexpected noises, smells, etc...."

—PTSD UK

Here's a news flash: No soldier gives his life. That's not the way it works. Most soldiers who make a conscious decision to place themselves in harm's way do it to protect their buddies. They do it because of the bonds of friendship - and it goes so much deeper than friendship.

—Eric Massa, brainyquote.com

13 through 16 May 2010: With Mr. Clean at the Wall—Band of Brothers, Part 10

Mr. Clean had never been to the "Wall" in Washington, so Randy and I remedied that and arranged for a mini-reunion in DC. Six former Mashers would converge on the Capital: Randy, Mr. Clean and I drove from North Carolina; and Richard Cross (Tricky Dick) from Allentown, Pennsylvania. Later that evening Lou Bartolotta would arrive from Philadelphia, and John "Timmy" Cleary from Pennsylvania.

***

On our first day, no one wanted to waste time, and the weather was comfortable, so Randy, Trick, and I escorted Mr. Clean to the Wall.

While riding the metro, Randy and I told Mr. Clean of our previous experiences at the memorial, hoping those stories would help prepare Mr. Clean for his impending encounter. He told us he had not gone before because so its black granite surface contained the names of so many friends and he didn't know if he could get through the experience.

When we arrived at the Memorial, we went through the registry but only found one of Mr. Clean's friends—elusive memories of names and their spellings had betrayed Mr. Clean. Then we walked down the brick walkway, descending along the Wall. We found Mr. Clean's friend and Bravo Good Dealers, who were killed in action. Mr. Clean fared well and was in control of his emotions, although he would later tell us he was on the verge of tears much of the time.

Later, while taking pictures at the statue of the three soldiers, a man about my age came up to me. His face was trembling, and he actually looked fearful "You flew Huey's?" he asked me, seeing the helicopter on my shirt.

"Roger that," I said.

The man swallowed hard and fought against the emotions boiling within him. He finally managed, "You guys saved my ass." His voice trembled, but he pointed towards the memorial and add, "I'd be on that wall if it weren't for you."

Knowing what the vet was feeling, I welled up, moved by this veteran's expression of gratitude. He took my hand and shook it. "Let it out. That's what you need."

He cried and looked at the ground, fighting for control of himself. His hand went to his face, and he rubbed his eyes. People standing nearby stopped to watch as Mr. Clean, Tricky and Randy came to my side.

"Every time I hear a helicopter … every time I hear that sound …" he said, unable to finish his thought.

"The whoppa whoppa whoppa," I said. "Yeah, I have to look up too."

"It takes me back."

Mr. Clean, Tricky and Randy made quick introductions, but this troubled vet's mind and heart were elsewhere. He really wasn't *listening* and began his retreat. "I just want to thank you guys for supporting us."

"No need to thank us—just doing our job," said Randy.

The vet waved and stepped away and blended into the crowd. Mr. Clean, Tricky, and Randy hovered closer to me and asked how the encounter began.

Again, the whoppa whoppa whoppa, the significance of the Huey hit home. The troubled veteran could not have made a more genuine gesture of appreciation for all helicopter pilots.

After visiting the Korean War Memorial, the four of us headed back to the hotel to welcome Timmy and Lou. We had dinner and retired to one of our rooms, where we drank and bullshat until midnight. Randy spiked my Mountain Dew with vodka.

The next day, we went to Arlington National Cemetery, where we visited the Tomb of the Unknown Soldier.

All the walking and heat took its toll on us, especially me with horrendous back pain. So, we headed back to the hotel. I relaxed while the other five guys returned to the wall and walked through the mall to the World War II Memorial. Tricky Dick returned to Allentown that evening.

The next day, the five of us piled into two cars and went to the Smithsonian's aviation museum, about twenty miles west of DC. The highlight included seeing the VTOL (Vertical Take-Off and Landing) aircraft, which Lou had actually flown while with Bell Helicopters.

That evening, Hugh, Mr. Clean's son, joined us. Hugh was a writer and college professor in North Carolina. Again, we stayed up late telling and re-telling war stories and listening intently to Mr. Clean, who offered a commander's take on things which was most enlightening.

The next morning Mr. Clean thanked us for being with him while at the wall. He was very glad to have completed one more mission. Both Mr. Clean and Timmy extended invitations for our next mini-reunion. We said goodbye and went our separate ways.

September 2010: Dear Mom—PTSD, Part 21

During a one-on-one session with my psychologist, Dr. Mako, I broached a heretofore topic that I had never raised. I was feeling guilty that I hadn't had a heart-to-heart conversation with Mom. There were questions I wanted to ask her, but I thought they were best left unspoken, as was anything about Vietnam. I wanted to know about her feelings during my flight training and combat tours. I also wanted to thank her for being supportive, even though I'm sure she was dying inside.

The author, and his Mom, Christmas, 1951 (Author's private collection).

Dr. Mako suggested I compose a letter to Mom, a way of making peace with myself, similar to the story he asked me to write about Dau Tran.

Dear Mom,

I have many questions and comments for you. I wish I had discussed them with you so many times and so many years ago, but I chose not to for fear of opening old wounds and causing you to relive the pain you endured during my years in the Army.

I now know PTSD hindered my ability to communicate. I'm not making excuses, but for thirty-five years I had psychological problems that I didn't even realize, couldn't recognize, and therefore, caused problems for me.

PTSD is difficult to understand, let alone explain, and it's something I will have to deal with for the rest of my life. I must continue to look at things in different ways, face my demons, and much more.

I know you didn't want me to enlist in the Army, especially with a war in progress halfway around the world. I can't imagine how you felt when I enlisted to be a helicopter pilot. Did you know how badly I wanted to fly and how much I would come to love it? Tell me about your feelings on that March morning at the train station when I left for basic training—I remember seeing you cry as the train pulled away.

How did you feel on that July evening when I called to tell you I had finally soloed in an OH-23? What were you feeling and thinking in February 1970, when I graduated from flight school and you pinned my bars on my shoulders? And what was going through your mind on the March morning when we said goodbye at the airport and I flew off to Vietnam. I remember hugging you and as I walked away you waved, and you were smiling.

Please understand, Mom, that I was answering my call to duty, just like the millions of Americans of your generation did during World War II.

Other questions would have come up in our conversation. Did you watch the six o'clock news every day? Did you understand the extent of my involvement in Cambodia and missions I flew every day? I want you to know I purposely said little about flying in my letters—didn't want to upset you.

I want you to know that I flew safely and rarely took unnecessary risks—unless the lives of Americans were at stake. I completed all of my missions to the best of my ability except for one which was totally unnecessary and suicidal (The battalion commander upheld my position and he commended me for making a good common-sense decision.) And yes, I goofed off from time to time but thankfully worked such shenanigans out of my system without cost.

I want to know how you served your three tours of duty. What was it like at home with the family, especially when Stevie enlisted and went to Germany? How did people treat you? What were Christmases like? Did you sleep well or were you haunted by dreams? Did you intuitively know anything?

Please know that I never wanted to bring you pain. Maybe it's good that I didn't tell you about what was really going on and how so many traumas from the war continue to affect me today. I've experienced things most people couldn't possibly understand, and I think about the war every day of my life—such was its intensity and its many memories that come forward to my mind's eye again and again.

Do you remember your birthday in 1973 when I sneaked into the house and surprised you? I'll never forget that—I can still feel you hugging me and the relief you expressed.

Did you ever want to ask me about Vietnam? It seems very few people wanted to do so or were afraid to do so? Did you suspect I had problems?

I cry a lot today, and that's good—all part of the healing process. When that happens, I know I'm dealing with my PTSD. I want you to know I've been getting help since 2006 and I have a great support system.

It's still very difficult and I regress from time to time, but I will get better and someday will find peace of mind and be able to grant total forgiveness—even for myself.

Today, if I could have one wish fulfilled, it would be to spend one day with you, holding you in my arms, talking and laughing, and telling you how lucky I was to have you as my Mom, and that I love you so very much.

With the greatest of love, your son,

Joe

"From the Halls of Montezuma, to the Shores of Tripoli;
We fight our country's battles in the air, on land, and sea;
First to fight for right and freedom and to keep our honor
clean;
We are proud to claim the title of UNITED STATES
MARINES...."

—"The Marines Hymn"[2]

24 January 2012: Dad Died Today

Dad had been battling dementia and Alzheimer's disease when sepsis infection slowly shut down his body's functions.

About four weeks ago, during one of my regular visits to the nursing home, I visited Dad to wish him a Merry Christmas. We talked a bit, and he opened the token gift I had brought to him, chocolate chip cookies—which he loved and wished he had more often. To pass the time, I'd sing a phrase or two from songs I knew Dad loved.

"Pardon me, boy, is that the ..."

Dad would light up, smile, point with a wagging finger at me and say, "Yeah, yeah, it'll come to me."

I then sang, "You leave the Pennsylvania Station about a quarter to four, read a magazine and you're in Baltimore."

"'Chattanooga Choo Choo,'" Dad said.

"Very good," I said. Then, after a few seconds, "Try this one." I sang, "Heavenly shades of night are falling—it's ..."

---

[2]—"The Marines Hymn" introduced by Francesco Maria Scala, originated by Jacques Offenback, 1867

Again. Dad would get excited and eventually come up with the correct title, "Twilight Time," by the Platters.

I threw a few more musical questions his way and then went on my way, leaving Dad in good spirits.

About two weeks later I was visiting Dad when the nurse entered his room and gave him a capsule, his afternoon medication. Dad put the capsule in his mouth, took a drink

of water and swallowed. After the nurse left the room, he spit the capsule onto the floor and grinned—an expression of sheer, gleeful defiance.

I suspected at that moment Dad would probably die within a few days. I spoke with the nurse just before leaving and she confirmed my suspicion. She also told me that Dad was refusing to eat. She explained that some people just know when their bodies betrayed and doomed them ... and they want to end it. "I've seen it time and time again," she said.

Dad's military awards and decorations, my gift to him, Christmas Eve, 2005 (Author's private collection).

***

On Tuesday morning, 24 January 2012, my sister Monica called me to tell me that Dad was near death. I immediately dressed and drove to the nursing home—about thirty minutes before my arrival Dad died. Uncle Al arrived shortly after me. He approached

Dad, held him by the shoulders, gave him a quick caress, puddled up and turned away. Within the hour, the funeral director arrived and most respectfully took Dad to the funeral home to prepare him for burial.

I helped my two sisters, Kathy and Monica, pack up Dad's possessions and straighten up his room. Then, as I was driving home, I called Lynda to cancel my dance lesson because of Dad's death. I broke down on the phone.

Dad's memorial service and viewing were held during the evening hours on Thursday, 26 January. The entire family and friends arrived to mourn and to celebrate Dad's life. Dad's little brother, Uncle Richie, drove in from Maryland with his daughter, Caroline, and it was very nice to see them.

At about seven o'clock, Lynda and some of my dance friends surprised me with their arrivals. This surprised me because Lynda always had group lessons on Thursday evenings, through nine o'clock. More surprising was in a matter of minutes over twenty of my dance friends were at the wake.

Dad was a member of the Marine Corps League. A dozen former Marines arrived, wearing their red blazers, and presented their last goodbye and salute to Dad. As they departed, I took the lectern for my eulogy. I got emotional but still got through my two minutes of remarks. I got emotional, especially when I read:

Today, I envision Dad in heaven, young and handsome, wearing his Marine Corps dress blue uniform. He's with Mom, who is simply beautiful, with her locks of red hair and a dress, one that she would have made—both flowing gracefully, as they glide effortlessly across heaven's dance floor, probably to a favorite song such as "Spanish Eyes" or a Glenn Miller tune, maybe "In the Mood."

Yes, they have been reunited and are in each other's arms again ... and they're dancing, clearing the dance floor again— even the angels step aside and marvel. They're together again, in each other's arms, rejoicing in their love and dancing for eternity.

Afterwards, Uncle Al, the new family patriarch, took command and called all family members and friends that were veterans and first responders to join him, forming a line in front of the casket. "Atten—tion," ordered Uncle Al.

He then read a few prepared remarks. When he finished, he said, "About face," followed by, "Present arms," and we saluted Staff Sergeant USMC, Stephen J. Sepesy, raising our right arms in a slow and respectful manner. Three seconds later, Uncle Al said, "Order arms," and we slowly lowered our salutes, honoring another veteran who had passed.

With the close of the memorial service, I thanked all of my friends for attending the service. I asked Lynda, "You had group classes this evening—why are you here?"

"This was more important," she answered. I pulled her close to me and embraced her.

I then introduced Lynda to my immediate family. During my introduction of Lynda to Uncle Richie, he told Lynda and me that the actions of my dance friends were a beautiful demonstration of love and respect. Lynda then excused herself, telling me that her group was off to dance at our usual Thursday evening club. I told Lynda that I would see her in a couple of days and to enjoy herself.

As Lynda left, Uncle Richie said, "You should go dance with your friends, Joe,"

"No, I can't do that—not now!"

"Now wait a minute. Your Mom and Dad were talented and beautiful dancers. What better way to honor them—go with your friends. It would mean a lot to everyone. Believe me."

I thanked Uncle Richie for his thoughts and suggestion and eventually changed my mind, joining with Lynda and two dozen of our dance friends for an hour and a half of dancing—and knowing that Mom and Dad were enjoying heaven's dance floor, smiling along with me and Lynda and our many dance friends.

Thank you, Uncle Richie!

The next day, my family gathered at the funeral home, formed our funeral procession and took Dad to the cemetery. The priest gave his final blessing and "Taps" was played. That song, that haunting but beautiful, that meaningful and singular song brought tears to my eyes. Both Mom and Dad were now gone—and my brothers and sisters were moving on to our next phases of life.

***

"Our flag's unfurled to every breeze, from dawn to setting sun; We have fought in every clime and place where we could take a gun; In the snow of far-off northern lands and in sunny tropic scenes; You will find us always on the job—the UNITED STATES MARINES.

Here's health to you and to our Corps which we are proud to serve; In many a strife we've fought for life and never lost our nerve; If the Army and the Navy ever look on Heaven's scenes; They will find the streets are guarded by UNITED STATES MARINES."

—"The Marines Hymn"

I want to thank each of you for your service to our Nation. I have served with each of you during my active career. All of you are the most reliable, dedicated, and giving people I have ever known. I am truly proud to have each of you as a part of my life.

We each share a common bond of closeness and dedication to each other that cannot be explained and/or understood by those who have never been associated with the military services. For those who do not understand this bond I will have to say they have never had an association with others ready at any moment to give their life for the man or woman standing beside them or the soldier on the ground whom we supported. This is the dedication I know each of you gave plus the hundreds and hundreds of others with whom we served during our careers.

God bless you and all those who have served and are currently serving. Further, let's not forget those men and women who gave their lives in defense of this nation and freedom.

—LTC Harold R. Fisher, US Army (Retired), 11 Nov 2009

1 July 2013: At Arlington National Cemetery—Band of Brothers, Part 11

John Goosman called me a couple of weeks ago. Human remains from his shoot-down, forty-three years ago, had been recovered from a border area of South Vietnam and Cambodia. They were to be buried in Arlington National Cemetery on 1 July 2013.

After a few subsequent phone calls, Randy Clark, Major Fisher, Goose and I agreed to attend the memorial services.

The four of us gathered in an Arlington hotel on 30 June. That evening we four Mashers attended a dinner where we met with family members of the deceased and Pentagon personnel assigned to assist those families. Throughout the evening, we conversed with the wife and daughter of Lieutenant Leslie Douglas, the aircraft commander on that fateful day. They had questions about their loved one—but also many questions about how we lived and flew during our tours of duty. They clung to our every word, and their tears flowed freely.

The four of us then attended a memorial service at the funeral home that handled the arrangements. One flag-draped coffin contained the remains of three soldiers. They had died together and they would rest in peace together. Lieutenant Douglas's remains had been interred in his home state of Mississippi.

Also in attendance were the current Commanding Officer and First Sergeant of the 227th Assault Helicopter Battalion of the 1st Cavalry Division, stationed at Fort Hood, Texas. These two soldiers considered our three fallen Skytroopers and us from 1970 as brothers in arms.

The CO presented a beautiful tribute to the fallen and elegantly expressed thoughts about our everlasting bond, that powerful and enduring connection known as the band of brothers. Randy and I sat next to one another, and we both cried.

Goose had commissioned a challenge coin to commemorate our four Mashers killed in action that last day of the Cambodian incursion. The back side presented the Bravo Good Deal patch. The front side presented the names of the four soldiers, the date of the incident, a Huey in flight, and the crest of the 227th AHB.

Goose gave a coin to members of the diseased families, Mr. Clean, Randy and me, and to the two current Skytroopers from Fort Hood.

Challenge coin designed by John Goosman, commemorating deaths of First Lieutenant Leslie Douglas, First Lieutenant Richard Dyer, Specialist 5 John Burgess, and Sergeant First Class Juan Diaz (Courtesy of John Goosman).

On the following morning, we gathered at the Ft. Meade chapel. Awaiting the casket and family and friends were; a horse-drawn caisson, the post's band, and an entire platoon of soldiers that served as honor guard.

The base's PX was directly across the street. The band played "Amazing Grace," as pall bearers removed the casket from the hearse. I watched people in the PX parking lot—they stopped, faced the chapel, stood silently and saluted—what a beautiful show of respect. I was already puddling up.

After a brief service, the casket was placed upon the caisson. While the band played another hymn, people within sight of the ceremony again stopped and saluted. When all was ready, the honor guard, band and caisson led the procession to the gravesite.

As the procession passed through the grounds' intersections, drivers of cars came to a halt, the occupants of the cars stepped out, stood in silence and saluted. The dignity and power of the moment burned into my memories and my heart. Never had I seen such displays of respect and understanding, patriotism and pride.

At the gravesite, last prayers and blessings were heard. The American flag atop the casket was folded and presented to one of the family members. A twenty-one-gun salute echoed across the cross-covered hills of Arlington, and "Taps" was played. Oh, my … "Taps" was played … and I cried.

The families experienced closure—after forty-three years, the last page had been turned, ending their loved ones' saga.

For Goose—I don't know if he will ever experience closure. I like to think that his mission involving his crew is now complete. But his personal mission, recovering from the trauma and achieving peace of mind, may never be fully resolved.

The four of us drove back to North Carolina, then our separate ways home. We discussed getting together again, unfortunately, that gathering of Mashers would not take place.

***

Rest in peace and may God bless Lieutenant Leslie Douglas, Lieutenant Richard Dyer, Specialist 5 John Burgess, and Sergeant First Class Juan Diaz.

Courage is the first of human qualities because it is the quality which guarantees the others.

—Aristotle

13 March 2015: Jackie Earns Her Wings

I flew to Denver, Colorado yesterday to attend my daughter's, graduation from the Frontier Airlines, Flight Attendants school. A month earlier Frontier hired Jacqueline Noelle and today was her big day.

After the usual preliminary addresses by airline instructors and management, the time for receiving wings arrived. Of the thirty-three graduates called for recognition, Jackie would number twenty-two. If called, a family member or friend could join a graduate in front of the office.

When Jackie's name was called, she received her wings and motioned for me to join her. She made lovely comments about me and my flying experiences—and I couldn't have been prouder of her, because of her poise and graciousness, respect and love. She had honored me, and I felt nothing but admiration and love for her. My little girl had truly grown up, overcoming more than her share of hurdles—and had succeeded.

Jackie handed me the wings, which I pinned to her blouse. We hugged, and I said, "I'm so proud of you and I love you very much."

After the ceremony, Jackie showed me around the classrooms and learning stations, which included an authentic section of a jetliner in which the students applied their lessons in a hands-on way. It was impressive. Jackie and I had a quick lunch and then I left, on my way back to the airport and home, so proud of my little girl.

***

Wings run in my family. Dad was a crew chief on US Marine Corps F-4U Corsairs in World War II, serving on Guadalcanal in the Pacific theater. Today, Jackie won her wings!

The challenge of leadership is to be strong, but not rude;
be kind, but not weak; be bold, but not bully; be thoughtful,
but not lazy; be humble, but not timid; be proud, but not
arrogant; have humor, but without folly.

—Jim Rohn, goodreads.com

30 October 2016: Mr. Clean Died Today— Band of Brothers, Part 12

For the past five years Major Fisher had been battling blood cancer, slogging through tests upon tests and exam after exam, hospital stays, and the usual physical and mental difficulties. Randy Clark helped the family during this time, helping to relieve the normal, mounting pressures being experienced by Major Fisher's two sons, Hugh and Justin.

At first Randy would make weekly visits to Mr. Clean, usually involving running errands and socializing, followed by a lunch or dinner. Those involved two-hour-round-trip drives for Randy.

When Mr. Clean was moved to the VA hospice, Randy helped Hugh and Justin prepare their dad's home for sale. When the end was nearing for Major Fisher, Randy visited him at the hospice every day and was nearby when he passed.

Randy had gone above and beyond as a care-giver for his former commanding officer. Their bond was unique and true. Not only was Randy one hell of a superb pilot—he was and is one hell of a great friend and human being.

On 4 and 5 November, Randy, Goose and I attended Mr. Clean's funeral services in North Carolina. On the evening of the 4th, we gathered at the Midway United Methodist Church in Kannapolis, North Carolina. Memorabilia that traced Mr. Clean's life was on display, covering a dozen eight-foot tables—special things that detailed his life from the days of his youth and schooling, through his military service and retirement.

The gathering was indeed a celebration of Mr. Clean's life. It was festive with a buffet of home-cooked meals provided by Mr. Clean's friends and fellow parishioners.

The celebration of his life included brief eulogies from family and friends. Randy, Goose and I stood at the lectern and told brief, personal stories about Mr. Clean's influence on our lives. Randy had the most trouble breaking down twice, but finished his remarks.

On the following day, family and friends accompanied the remains of Harold Fisher to his last church service and resting place. At the cemetery, we spoke our last goodbyes and shed more tears. A twenty-one-gun salute echoed across the chilled landscape ... and then "Taps" was played. As usual, tears streamed down my cheeks.

Mr. Clean's ashes were placed at the gravesite of his wife. Justin produced for interment, with his dad's ashes, a miniature bottle of Royal Crown Whisky, Mr. Clean's favorite and omni-present, sipping beverage. Randy, Goose and I saluted Major Fisher one last time, then left.

Our band of brothers was dwindling and now our leader was gone, and our own mortality became more apparent to us. Damn! I was sixty-six years old, hoping my best years were still ahead. Our Masher trio said goodbye and departed until our next gathering.

Rest in peace, Major Harold Fisher "Mr. Clean" and Masher 6—one great man, aviator and warrior ... and friend. I miss you.

Older men declare war. But it is the youth that must fight and die.

—Herbert Hoover, 27 June 1944

"During the air war of 1944, a four-man combat crew of a B-17 bomber took a vow to never abandon one another no matter how desperate the situation. The aircraft was hit by flak during a mission and went into a terminal dive, and the pilot ordered everyone to bail out. The top turret gunner obeyed the order, but the ball turret gunner discovered that a piece of flak had jammed his turret and he could not get out. The other three men in his pact could have bailed out with the parachutes, but they stayed with him until the plane hit the ground and exploded. They all died."

—Sebastian Junger, *War*, published by Twelve, 2010

Youth—Band of Brothers, Part 13

Such a significant part of my life, sharing the experiences of war with my band of brothers—are matchless, and I will never forget them as long as I live!

Beginning on two preceding pages, from left to right, Masher Aircraft Commanders:

Line 1; CW2 Troy "Pig" Wise and CW2 Melvin "Cecil" Strobel,

Line 2; CW2 John "Cuddles" Codling and CW2 Lou "the Godfather" Bartolotta,

Line 3; Trent "Fang" Munsey and the author CW2 Joe "Jo3y" Sepesy;

Line 4; Captain Julius "Julie" Duval and Captain Richard Beck, and,

Line 5: Statues at the Vietnam War Memorial: Three Soldiers, dedicated on Veterans Day 1984; and the Nurses, dedicated on Veterans Day 1993 (Author's private collection).

Perspective will come in retrospect.

—Melody Beattie,inspiringquotes.us

Believe you can and you're halfway there.

—Theodore Roosevelt

** Dance **

"May I have this dance?"

—Joseph Michael Sepesy, "The Most Beautiful Invitation," from *Word Dances II, Your Time to Dance,* Lulu Press, 2014

"My past has not defined me, destroyed me, deterred me, or defeated me; it has only strengthened me."

—Steve Maraboli, *Unapologetically You: Reflections on Life and the Human Experience,* A Better Today, May 2013

EPILOGUE

Final Thoughts: Flight, PTSD, Life … and Dance

In a memoir, your main contract with the reader is to tell the truth, no matter how bizarre.

—Edmund White

** Dance **

"Dance with me—let the joy begin."

—Joseph Michael Sepesy, "Elation," from *Word Dances,*
A Collection of Verses and Thoughts about
Ballroom Dancing, Lulu Press, 2014

A Transformed Life

Dancing

Dancing has been transformative for me. It has been the major factor in facing my PTSD equation. I know my PTSD will never go away and will continue to affect me, and dance has improved the quality of my life immeasurably. I will continue to dance four or five times a week, including lessons, twice a week—the learning and the music will never end. And, when I'm gone, I want people to have a party and dance to my favorite songs and remember me on the dance floor having the time of my life.

Dancing is a passion that is sated by the beautiful and demanding music of multiple genres of ballroom music as described below and within the last pages of this memoir. My books about ballroom dancing are proof of that passion.

Writing

Lynda has inspired me to where I have written four books about ballroom dancing: *Word Dances, A Collection of Verses and Thoughts about Ballroom Dancing; Word Dances II, Your Time to Dance; Word Dances III, Celebration; a*nd *Word Dances IV, The Romance of the Dance. Word Dances V* will be published in 2021. I've also written a historical novel, set in World War I, *The Relic of Domremy* and its sequel, *The Flight of St. Joan's Cross, The Relic of Domremy, Part II*.

With the publishing of my *Word Dances* series, Lynda and I have appeared on local television. Dancing is the theme, but the story is enhanced with discussion about how I overcame physical problems and PTSD. Articles have also appeared about me and Lynda in the *Youngstown Vindicator*, other local newspapers, and the national magazine, *The American Dancer*.

The Department of Veterans Affairs

I thank my fellow veterans from the PTSD group and my doctors for their help and support.

Thank you, Terese Hurin, my most capable orthotist at the Canton, Ohio, VA clinic. Terese has worked with me for four years, patiently applying her skills by providing me with leg braces that have complemented my life style. She has devised braces I can wear with both street shoes and dance shoes. Terese has enabled me to maintain my passion—ballroom dancing and without her expertise, I would probably be an incomplete person.

The VA also out-sourced me to medical specialists with whom I had already established doctor-patient relationships. Those referrals were for seven operations on my neck, shoulder, and eyes.

** Dance **

"Pilot and Dancer, Dance Flight, the Waltz, Part 2"

Silver wings earned in the summer of life, in the
winter of '70, and onto Asian jungles, paddies,
and mountains.
        Silver wings earned in the autumn of life, in 2011,
        in studios and in American dance palaces.

Silver wings inspired by stars and stripes, beneath
thumping rotor blades, above the din and fury of
battle.

> Silver wings inspired by music, floating across
> lustrous dance floors to the sound of beautiful
> three-four music.

Silver wings in a place of war and death, in
combat flight's chaos and fright.

> Silver wings in a place of music's life and its
> touch, with dance flight's hold and joy.

Silver wings with dedicated and skilled aircrews
wearing olive drab, the loss of friends and
comrades.

> Silver wings while holding ladies in golden
> gowns, in the company of new friends and so
> many dances.

Silver wings attacked, with injury and scars, with
unseen wounds and the horrors of battle that
haunt.

> Silver wings with lingering pain and a lasting
> limp, but ways to cope, overcome, and succeed.

Silver wings from the age of nineteen, now
displayed with awards and photos, but still with
demon dreams at night.

> Silver wings at the age of sixty-one, now with
> every step and every dance and sweet memories
> that abound.

Silver wings, from the guidance and care of
knowing veterans, protective and experienced.

> Silver wings from the guidance and love of a
> knowing teacher, talented and passionate.

Two lives, separate and apart, yet two lives very
much in common—bound by the silver wings of
... a pilot and dancer.

Inspiration

Yes, this is a strange title for a verse in a book
primarily about ballroom dancing. But this odd
coupling has everything to do with my life's many
transitions: from high school student to US Army
flight student; then in combat as a helicopter pilot
in Vietnam to inner-city school teacher, labor
advocate, and union official; through PTSD's
devastation, counseling, and recovery; the daily
challenges of family and parenting; many
physical setbacks—surviving all, eventually, to
write and dance.

I love the fact that I have earned two sets of
silver wings—the first in February 1970 with my
warrant-officer bars. Mom pinned my bars on,
and Dad pinned my wings on. The second, when
Lynda showed me dance flight with a waltz in
May 2011.

We both wear small sterling rings in the
shape of wings to remember that moment....
—Joseph Michael Sepesy, "Pilot and Dancer,
Dance Flight, the Waltz, Part 2," from
Word Dances II, Your Time to Dance,
Lulu Press, 2015

"There is no such thing as closure for soldiers who have survived a war. They have an obligation, a sacred duty, to remember those who fell in battle beside them all their days and to bear witness to the insanity that is war."

—Harold G. Moore, Joseph L. Galloway, *We Are Soldiers Still: A Journey Back to the Battlefields of Vietnam*, Harper, 2008

Veterans Day, 2017: You Could Hear a Pin Drop—PTSD, Part 22

A young dancer, a student at Lynda's dance studio, asked me to visit her seventh-grade class on Veterans Day to discuss the Vietnam War, my PTSD, and how ballroom dancing was the impetus for improving the quality of my life. Without thinking, I agreed. A minute later, I wasn't sure about participating. But Mina was a good kid, and her involvement in front of her classmates would make her feel very good about herself.

About a week before the visit, Mina's teacher informed me I would not speak to her class—I would speak before two assemblies: the first, before the entire 7th grade and parents; then a repeat assembly before the entire 8th grade and parents. *Hmm,* I thought, *okay, I'm committed, I'll get through it—I hope.*

I spoke with Mina and told her about my idea for ending both presentations—we would dance an East Coast Swing to a popular and recognizable song to show the joy of ballroom dancing—even for someone wearing braces and using a cane for balance and safety. Now all I had to do was prepare a twenty-minute talk.

I prepared the usual type of speech given by any veteran—all about training, units, and a few experiences—much of which would make little sense to most of the listeners. I had heard plenty in my day and I usually found them too long, which led to boredom because the vet didn't know when to end his tale.

The more I reviewed my speech, the more I disliked it. So, I changed my entire approach and focused on pulling the *kids* into my experiences. If I could make my words relevant to them, at their level, my discussion would be of greater value and a more effective learning experience. But how could I make the military and war relevant to kids, thirteen to fifteen years old?

I arrived at the school at the appointed time, wearing my dress blues and Cavalry Stetson. I met with Mina's teacher to discuss the agenda, then the principal who got me settled in the auditorium.

As the students, parents and teachers filed into the auditorium, I briefed Mina about the agenda and reassured her that the finale, our dance, would be fantastic, "Just enjoy the steps we've danced before—I know you're a good follower, smile and have a ball. You're beautiful!" Mina was excited.

The principal introduced me by reading the resume of my military service. Then, I hobbled forward and awkwardly climbed the eight steps onto the stage, to the lectern, and I began. Excerpts of my speech and how I respond follow.

"Ladies and gentlemen, millions of American men and women have served in our country's military … millions. Hundreds of thousands have been wounded or killed during their time of service … that is hundreds of thousands. Such staggering numbers can be hard to grasp and put into perspective, especially through the eyes of students of your age and experiences.

Today, I'd like to personalize a message. I want you to feel what it would be like to know a veteran who goes off to war, therefore better understand why we celebrate Veterans Day.

Today we celebrate Veterans Day. That's a special day for Americans, to varying degrees. For young men and women, such as yourselves; it's a different day of school because your routine has been changed, less bookwork, because of this assembly. For other Americans it is a time to remember, to laugh and to cry, to think about the brave men and women who have served in the Army, Navy, Marine Corps, Air Force, Coast Guard, Reserves and National Guard. Again, today, I hope I can deepen your understanding of what being a veteran is all about.

We're going to talk about 3 vets. Their names are Gary, Butch, and Jeff. Now, in your own minds, picture three young men ... or women. For the purpose of this discussion; Gary is the kid next door, Butch is a high school buddy here in Austintown, and Jeff is your brother or cousin. Also, for the purpose of this discussion: all three decide to enlist in the US Army, and all three enter flight training. They are hoping to become helicopter pilots.

After training, you and your family send them off with a goodbye party and there they go to basic training and flight school One year later, they make their successful return to home, before going to war. They are now Warrant Officers with silver bars and wings on their uniforms. You note they seem different ... more serious, to say the least. After a two-week leave, they are sent to war. Everyone says goodbye and wishes them the best and a safe return.

Now stop—let's put on hold the story of Gary, Butch, and Jeff. Let's jump into a time machine and consider this same set of circumstances happening:

From 1991 to the Present: Three other young soldiers are sent to the War in Iraq and Afghanistan.

1964-1973: Three other young soldiers are sent to the Vietnam War.

1950-1953: Three other young soldiers are sent to the Korean War.

1941-1945: Three other young soldiers are sent to World War II.

1917-1918: Three other young soldiers are sent to World War I.

And don't forget the millions who served but did not see war.

What I want you to know is—what's going on with you now and with our imaginary trio of Gary, Butch and Jeff is nothing new. It's been the case for all wars in which Americans have fought.

Okay, we're done with time traveling.

So, Gary, Butch, and Jeff are sent to Vietnam after their goodbyes from family and friends.

Three weeks later, you are surprised to hear that Gary, the kid next door, has been wounded. He's okay, but his time of service in war is over.

Five months later you hear that Butch, the high school kid, has been killed in action."

My voice trembles, and I tear up.

"Butch returns home in a flag-draped coffin. Services are held, a 21-gun salute rings out, and a bugler plays 'Taps.'"

Now, I'm crying and struggling to speak—but determined to finish my talk.

"Another three weeks go by and you are shocked to hear that your brother, Jeff, has been killed in action. You, your parents, family and friends openly cry and grieve their loss. Jeff returns home in a flag-draped coffin. Services are held, a 21-gun salute rings out, and a bugler plays, 'Taps.'"

Again, I must speak deliberately and more slowly, tears are flowing freely.

"Ladies and gentlemen, I hope that experiencing such imaginary stories about Gary, Butch and Jeff has enhanced your lives. You will never be the same because now, you truly understand what being a veteran is all about—that is serving in uniform, serving your country, the USA … and in some cases, sacrificing for your country, because freedom isn't free … it never has been … it never will be."

I am now calm and speaking normally.

"Okay, your exercise is over.

Let me tell you about the real Gary, Butch and Jeff. In 1968, those three young men and I did enlist in the US Army, did complete helicopter flight school and did serve in the Vietnam War. Gary and I were assigned to the same combat unit with the 1st Cavalry Division. (Watching the movie, *They Were Soldiers Once … and Young* would give you a clear image about the Vietnam War, and what flying helicopters in combat was all about.)

We were in country only three weeks when Gary got shot—half of his left leg was blown away. Later, we counted 150 bullet holes in his Huey helicopter. Thankfully, only one hit Gary, but it was enough to end his time in war … in Vietnam.

Two months later, Jeff was flying a gunship, covering a flight of Hueys landing to an LZ, a landing zone … a hot landing zone. Jeff was shot through the arm—a clean in-and-out would. He convalesced in Japan for a month and was told he would be going home.

Jeff said, 'No, I want to return to my unit and keep on flying.' So, Jeff did return to his unit and continued to fly."

Here, I choke up again.

"Three months later, Butch, who was my roommate during flight school, was running a combat assault against an enemy position. He was shot through the mouth and died two days later.

Butch returned home in a flag-draped coffin. Services were held, a 21-gun salute rang out … and a bugler played 'Taps.'"

My voice trembles again, and I'm gasping and crying.

> "Two weeks after Butch's death, Jeff was flying close cover support for another assault flight and was shot literally between the eyes. He died instantly.
>
> Jeff returned home in a flag-draped coffin. Services were held, a 21-gun salute rang out ... and a bugler played 'Taps.'"

I stop—take out my handkerchief to dry my eyes and take a drink of water. I glance to my right—the principal is crying. To my left—members of the choir who are sitting on the floor of the stage are staring at me. I notice two girls are crying. You could hear a pin drop. I continued.

> "I frequently think about Gary, Butch, and Jeff. We helped one another get through flight school; we goofed off, told stories and joked. Now I recall those moments, and sometimes I nod and smile ... sometimes I cry."

I exhale deeply, pause, and continue.

> "But what happened to me, you might be wondering. One week after Gary had his lower left leg blown off. I was shot down."

I don't elaborate on the shoot-down except for the injury to my back and subsequent problems. I speak briefly about flying helicopters and a couple of other mishaps. Then I broach the topic of PTSD.

> "Concerning my PTSD: I have demon dreams; sudden and loud noises cause me to lower myself and cover my head; I still have a foxhole mentality when certain situations arise ... and more.
>
> I still go to therapy at the VA clinic. I still cry, especially when I hear 'Taps' played. I get bummed out when I think too much about some experiences ... the worst ones, or when one of my PTSD

triggers gets the better of me. Forgive me if emotion gets to me during this presentation. That's just the way it is.

So, how do I cope?

I write books. I've published five books with three more to go in the next two years, including my Vietnam memoir. And most importantly ... I dance. Yes, even with braces and a cane, I can dance. I have learned 13 ballroom dances—I actually dance better than I walk. Go figure. The doctors can't explain why ... but I do dance better than I walk. And I'm going to prove that to you right now.

With some help, I am going to demonstrate an East Coast Swing dance to a very popular song. This is how you dance to rock 'n' roll, ballroom style. You'll recognize the song as soon as it begins.

But I need a partner. I'd like to introduce my friend, Mina Tokes. She is an excellent dancer for having had lessons for just a few months."

Mina and I then dance for two-and-a-half minutes and the audience loved it, giving us a standing ovation. I loved the moment for Mina. She danced confidently and joyfully!

"And lastly, after hearing this brief report, which is a mere scratching of the surface of hundreds of more thoughts and stories— some wonder, would I do it again? 'Yes! And, when that beautiful American flag is within sight, that yes becomes an absolutely, yes!'

When you leave here today, remember Gary, Butch and Jeff. That may cause you to think about the millions of other American veterans who are remembered and honored on this day. That may cause you to think about the American military men and women fighting for you and the USA at this very moment as we are gathered here.

I thank you and the Austintown school district, Ms. Keown, Mina Tokes and you for your attention! God bless America!"

All throughout, you could hear a pin drop … then applause.

** PTSD **

When you can tell your story and it doesn't make you cry, you know you have healed.

—Karen Salmansohn, declutteryourmind.com

Good writing is remembering detail. Most people want to forget. Don't forget things that were painful or embarrassing or silly. Turn them into a story that tells the truth.

—Paula Danzinger

** Dance **

"On the brink of decision ... at the edge of the floor ... take that last step of a danceless life and fall into the enchanting embrace of the music, now set free to enjoy ... to dance."

—Joseph Michael Sepesy, "Choosing Wisely," from *Word Dances, a Collection of Verses and Thoughts about Ballroom Dancing,* 2014

Mistakes and Regrets

Mistakes

I should have gone in the Army during the summer of 1968, not waiting to complete a quarter at Kent State University—to hell with that hundred-fifty-dollar scholarship. I realize that would have disrupted the time continuum that now exists—and who knows how my life would have changed.

I should have reported to the flight surgeon on the day of my shoot-down, 18 April 1970. I should have at least told him about the tightness and tingling and told him I could still fly without trouble. He would have established a record of the injury that I would need years later. But what's a dumbass new guy like me know?

I should have kept a more-detailed logbook, my maps, and every official military document I ever received.

I should have kept a journal and taken more pictures. I would have remembered more details and easily referenced during the writing of this memoir.

I should have learned more about the Vietnamese culture and taken time simply to observe.

I should have asked for the name of the soldier that died in the arms of LTC Galvin on my bird.

I should have known more about the military structure beyond the battalion level

I should have gone to Bangkok and Taiwan for R&R, instead of Hong Kong and Sydney, Australia twice—to experience more of the world.

I should have taken control of the bird from Wilk on the morning of 8 July 1970, should have told Dennehy to stop throwing flare fuses, should have climbed to altitude and told Wilk to go to hell.

I should have pursued a career in aviation, not education.

I should have stayed in touch with other members of my band of brothers such as Fish and Fang, Hermie, Cuddles, and Julie.

Regrets

Bravo 227 should have had group pictures taken.

The aviators of Bravo 227 should have received narratives with their awards, not nondescript template paragraphs that simply validated the awards.

The 1st Cav should have received the Presidential Unit Citation for action in Cambodia. Nixon's administration didn't have the balls to recognize our actions for political reasons, and the recommendation for the award was down-graded to a Valorous Unit Citation.

Reality

The USA should have settled for nothing less than a complete accounting and return of our POWs. President Nixon and Henry Kissinger knew the NVA did not return hundreds of American servicemen. The North Vietnamese never trusted the Nixon administration to pay reparation—a few billion dollars, as promised by Nixon in a secret letter. Payment never occurred—POWs were not released.

There were two separate tracks the North used to keep its POWs. Those tracks never crossed, so one group of POWs never encountered the other group. Hell, even North Vietnamese officials have admitted to this and more!

Presidential administrations have dodged the POW issue for decades, subverted efforts to resolve the issue, ignored it, and played with words. And the topper involved Senators Kerry of Massachusetts, and McCain of Arizona, both Vietnam vets. They hammered the last nail in the coffin of the POW issue when they both served on a congressional committee that addressed the POWs and MIAs (Missing in Action).

Those political hypocrites not only maintained the status quo on POWs, they also ordered the destruction of all evidence relevant to POWs after submitting the same bullshit report every other politician had submitted in previous years about POWs and MIAs. They cited not enough evidence, unreliable sources, con games, etc.

Their staff workers have testified, written books and held interviews, speaking to this travesty—and nothing happened. The media dropped the ball by not pursuing the issue with resolve. When asked about their committee's work, some smoke-screened, lied, angered and acted in a repugnant manner by belittling and reprimanding all who challenged them.

Both Kerry and McCain ran for president. They are heroes in the eyes of many. But how does one justify their unconscionable actions against our country's POWs and MIAs? Hell has special places for those who betray their fellow military men and women.

Living with this betrayal causes me great anger—perhaps the reason forgiveness of myself and others is so damned difficult. Whenever I hear their names, I am reminded of their most grievous sins committed against their fellow Americans.

There are dozens of books and many websites about the POW and MIA controversy. Some tell us about the crime of abandoning our POWs and falling short of a full accounting of our MIAs. Other authors tell us such positions are speculative or nothing more than conspiracy theories, even mythological. The books and reports I have read are voluminous, with evidence that confirms hundreds of our men were not released and remain in captivity.

I believe the evidence is overwhelming. I have presented a list of reading material in the appendix—some entries support my beliefs and will blow your minds. And know—you may not like what you read about our leaders going all the way back to World War II.

Dance

I kick myself for not learning how to dance until I was fifty-nine years old—I kick myself! But that all changed on 2 December 2009.

** Dance **

"I came, I saw, I danced."

—Joseph Michael Sepesy, "Choosing Wisely, Part 2" from *Word Dances III, Celebration*, Lulu Press, 2016

It took me a lifetime to become the person I am, to be ready for you.

—Linda Sepesy, my bride's mantra, 25 March 2018

** Dance **

"The most beautiful reason for dancing … is in your arms."

—Joseph Michael Sepesy "Beauty and the Dance," from *Word Dances, a Collection of Verses and Thoughts about Ballroom Dancing,* Lulu Press, 2014

Spring, 2018: Final Puzzle Pieces

It took me sixty-seven years to experience genuine love—that happened on 25 March—when Linda Deitrick-Rios and I kissed for the first time. It was magical!

Linda is a retired nurse and hospice volunteer, the mother of four and grandmother of thirteen—and, of course, excluding Lynda, my dance teacher, she is the best dancer I have ever led.

From the day of our first date, both of us discovered much commonality. Holding hands came so naturally, and as I would discover shortly thereafter, saying "I love you," would come just as easily. As we spent more time together and grew closer, I knew we would marry and the last piece of my life's puzzle would complete the picture.

***

Linda and I had been dating for several weeks. She and her friends from her Cuyahoga Falls dance club, the Ohio North Coast Jitterbug Connection, joined me and my A

Time to Dance friends at the Avon Oaks Ballroom in Girard, Ohio. As usual, my *Word Dances* books were displayed on the serving island next to our tables.

One of Linda's friends from her club, read the back cover of one book on display, saw my picture and name. The name stood out much more than the picture. Surprised, he said to his lady friend, "Hey! I know this guy! I thought he was dead—killed in Vietnam!"

The author escorts the lovely lady of dance, Linda Deitrick Rios, to a Christmas dinner-dance in 2018. (Author's private collection).

The lady friend pointed to me as Linda and I were returning to our table from the dance floor. The man that suddenly recognized me and said, "Joe! Joe Sepesy, do you remember me?"

I looked at the man and didn't have a clue. Then he said, "I'm Delbert Stewart. We enlisted in the Army with its buddy program in 1968."

"Well, I'll be damned," I said.

Delbert and I met at Kent State University in Air Force ROTC classes, knew college wasn't for either of us, and enlisted in the US Army for its Warrant Officer Flight Training program.

In December 1968 we went to Cleveland, Ohio to enlist. We completed basic training, and reported to Fort Wolters, Texas, for flight training. But Delbert had injured one of his knees during basic and re-injured it upon our arrival at Wolters. He could not continue with flight training but would report to Medic school. We never saw one another to say goodbye. After two years of service, Delbert received his honorable discharge.

Delbert and I sat and talked for a while, both knowing we had a lot of catching-up to do and enjoyed the rest of the evening, dancing and with bits and pieces of conversation throughout. But here's the cool part.

Delbert was a long-time member of the ONCJC. I had attended their dances in Cuyahoga Falls intermittently, beginning in 2015. I would go alone and sit in the same seat at the rear of the floor. Delbert always sat three seats to my left. We never spoke—never really paid attention to one another—dancing being the priority.

Then our paths crossed at Avon Oaks—this time in a much more meaningful and delightful way. Our story of reunion became the hot topic of discussion for both dance contingencies—an incredible coincidence—but more so, one incredible story.

PTSD is sadness, guilt, loneliness, isolation, despair, anger, fear, pain, confusion—the list is different for everyone affected. What PTSD isn't … is hopeless.

—PTSD Maxim during group therapy

2019: Living with PTSD: PTSD Part 23

My PTSD will never go away. I have accepted that and understand why I am the way I am—and that's a good thing.

My symptoms of PTSD have included survivor guilt and shame (traumatic guilt); anger, depression and stress; emotional numbing; mistrust of, and confrontation with figures of authority; withdrawal and avoidance; hypervigilance and hyperarousal; demon dreams and intrusive memories; and trauma reminders (anniversary dates of trauma, certain sounds, and other cues), and the big one—sensitivity to injustice.

Today my persistent symptoms include survivor guilt and shame; mistrust of, and confrontation with figures of authority; hyperarousal, demon dreams and intrusive memories; black and white thought processes versus shades of grey; and the big one—sensitivity to injustice.

My triggers include loud noises or unexpected noises of any volume, crowds in which my movements are restricted or blocked; others displaying incompetence; hearing "Taps" and military scenes on TV or in movies, and the actions of management that I perceive as unjust or threatening.

***

I wish I had known about PTSD decades ago. I wish I had understood why I thought, spoke and acted how I did—or at least had known what was influencing my life. Today, it seems I missed out on so much of life, could have been happier, and could have made better decisions. Such is hindsight.

Since early 2006, the quality of my life has improved considerably. Learning about PTSD and how to cope with it has made all the difference. Beginning ballroom dancing and writing has enhanced my life. Retirement after thirty-one, ridiculous years of teaching and divorce have been actions with positive and helpful results.

Concerning my physical condition despite many operations, titanium implants, chronic pain, advancing nerve damage, and orthopedic braces, I remain very active with ballroom dancing. Mindful eating and a regimen of exercises have fostered a loss of forty-five pounds—the mirror is friendly to me and my calendar is full.

For the record, I have had four lower back operations, two neck operations and two shoulder replacements—all directly related to my shoot down in April 1970.

But most of all, my life's missing puzzle piece was about to be put into place, completing a life's mural.

** PTSD **

While researching this memoir I came across maxims, verses, sayings—many profound thoughts relevant to PTSD. I find them most helpful in continuing my understanding of PTSD. Consider the following words of wisdom and share them with someone you suspect may need to hear them.

"According to Hoge and colleagues (2007), the key to reducing stigma is to present mental health care as a routine aspect of health care, similar to getting a check-up or an X-ray. Soldiers need to understand that stress reactions-difficulty sleeping, reliving incidents in your mind, and emotional detachment-are common and expected after combat... The soldier should be told that wherever they go, they should remember that what they're feeling is 'normal and it's nothing to be ashamed of.'"

—Joan Beder, *Advances in Social Work Practice with the Military,* Routledge, 2012

** Dance **

"The Joy of Dance"

"A celebration with lyrics and melody, a reason for rhythm and tempo,

A picture of bliss and charm, a place of togetherness and sharing,

A story through song and dreams, a moment of motion and magic.

A gift for now and always, a memory to embrace and hold dear.

A journey of sight and sound, a flight of delight for body and mind,

A time for smiles and harmony, for romance with that special someone.

All these things ... they are the joy of dance."

—Joseph Michael Sepesy, "The Joy of Dance," from *Word Dances, a Collection of Verses and Thoughts about Ballroom Dancing,* 2014

"I promise to dance with you always … and in all ways.

I promise to love you always … and in all ways.

To you, I make these … my promises."

—Joseph Michael Sepesy, "My Promises," from *Word
    Dances IV, the Romance of the Dance,* Lulu
    Press, 2014

19 October 2019: Linda and I Are Married

In 2016, I met the lovely Linda Deitrick-Rios on a dance floor. A romance and love affair blossomed, and we married on 19 October 2019. We combined our resources and watched the construction of our dream condo. It has everything we wanted, including a dance area that accommodates our needs. Linda is the best thing ever to happen to me. See is my angel, sent from heaven. She is my song and dance, my reason and life. I love her dearly!

***

On 8 September 2018, I surprised Linda with a proposal and ring at Lynda Styles' A Time to Dance studio in front of sixty friends. I had help in setting up the scenario and keeping it a secret from Linda. Delbert Stewart and Lynda were in on the plan.

After Lynda announced a phony spotlight dance to which Linda and I danced a rumba, I maneuvered Linda toward a chair that Lynda had placed toward the middle of the floor. I told her Lynda wanted to take our picture. Lynda then, surreptitiously, handed me the mic. I said, "My lovely Lady Linda, you danced into my life, then you danced into my heart. Now, together and forever, would you marry me?"

That blew Linda away, and after she expressed great surprise and much happiness, said, "Yes!" When the room calmed down, both of us made brief remarks. After I explained how the set-up occurred, Linda took the mic and said, "I could not ask for a more wonderful man. It is my pleasure, and it is my joy to dance with him and walk by his side."

Linda loves her rings, antique solitaires. I love my ring; two white-gold wings caressing one another.

***

Linda and Joe Sepesy, married 19 October 2012 (Author's private collection).

We were planning for 250 guests to attend our wedding celebration on 19 October 2019. We both love October. And God and mother nature blessed us with a perfect mid-autumn day.

Linda's matron of honor was friend and fellow nurse, Bennie Rock. My best man was Masher 2-2, Randy Clark. We married at St. Michael church, in Canfield, Ohio. The ceremony was brief and beautiful: we exchanged rings and read our own vows. Both of us choked up a bit. Then after the formal vows and exchanging of rings, pictures were taken in the church followed by a delicious, four-entrée buffet dinner with all the side dishes. Of course, music played in the background and a few friends danced intermittently during the meal.

Linda and I introduced guests of honor, and made brief comments. She introduced Bennie, who spoke beautifully about us falling in love, including beautifully placed Italian phrases. Randy also spoke, entertaining the group with humorous comments about our friendship, flight school and flying helicopters together, nearly fifty years ago with Bravo, 227.

I spoke about our dance instructor, Lynda Styles, thanking her for teaching me how to dance and going the extra mile regarding my physical problems.

Another guest of honor, justifiably recognized, was my orthotist, Terese Hurin. Without her expertise and persistence, I would have trouble walking—let alone dancing. Terese is now a student of ballroom dancing.

Rounding out our guests of honor were my daughter, Jackie, and John Goosman, another Vietnam vet that served with me in Bravo Company. John, a Bravo 227, door gunner, flew in from California to attend the wedding.

At six o'clock, the other 125 guests began arriving. It was a good thing that Linda and I planned two buffets. And the hall's manager rolled out more tables and chairs because within the first hour 350 people filled the hall, most of whom danced and danced the night away. At one point, Linda pulled me close and said, "I didn't know we knew so many people."

The gathering amazed the priest and security officers just as much—telling Linda and me they had never seen a reception quite like ours—so many people were dancing song after song, and no one displayed drunkenness or obnoxious behavior.

It is a tradition in the Youngstown, Ohio area to have a cookie table at weddings. Ours was thirty-two feet long and loaded with dozens and dozens of cookies and kolachis, baked by so many of our friends.

And there was the music and the dancing, music with leg-pulling dance-ability, beautiful melodies with definite rhythms and tempos—some with significance for those in attendance, such as a few songs made famous by local bands we knew in our younger years. Lynda volunteered to be the disc-jockey and played four hours of ballroom music and line dances that Linda and I had planned—thus keeping everyone happy.

Joe and Linda perform their wedding dance, a bolero. (Author's private collection).

The author's favorite wedding picture—just look at my beautiful bride! I'm a lucky guy! (Author's private collection).

After about an hour, Linda and I performed our wedding dance, a bolero to Celine Dion's *Falling into You*. We had performed it before an audience before and were ready. We danced it flawlessly, with joy, and with a slightly different ending—

we danced toward a chair on which I sat, leading Linda to me. I placed her on my lap and we kissed passionately. The crowd roared its approval, and we received a standing ovation.

I did not want the evening to end—such was the joy, the guests and food, the music and dancing. In retrospect, we should have planned for another hour of dancing.

***

Months later, family and friends are still commenting about our wedding. It was a throw-back and traditional for members of my family, conjuring memories from our youthful days. For others, it was a joyous evening of celebration.

Four months later, in February 2020, Linda and I celebrated as honeymooners and the wedding of our dance instructor Lynda and her fiancé, Jon Styles, on a cruise ship for twelve days through the Caribbean Sea and Panama Canal.

***

Retirement is fine, and life with Linda is exquisite.

My days go by—writing and dancing keep me active. I enjoy reading and watching the History Channel and the Cleveland Indians keep me entertained. Also, I never refuse the occasional nap. Linda, my bride, and I have much in common and we spend most of our time together. Life is good.

** Dance **

"Partners"

"They welcome their song of inspiration and take pleasure in it. Now everything will be to the music's end.

One leads, and one follows—yet they are equal in task, complementing the other while expressing the joy of movement.

He presents her, and she creates the beauty—their every step, each touch and look, paints a story with motion.

They feel their music, express it … and delight in the sound as their every nuance embellishes the dance. They cherish their art and wander with it … on the floor.

They play the music as much as any musician who conjures it. They become the music, its body and soul, its heartbeat and passion … its vision … its reason.

They are … partners."

—Joseph Michael Sepesy, "Partners," from *Word Dances, a Collection of Verses and Thoughts about Ballroom Dancing*, Lulu Press, 2014

"Recovery unfolds in three stages. The central task of the first stage is the establishment of safety. The central task of the second stage is remembrance and mourning. The central focus of the third stage is reconnection with ordinary life."

—Judith Lewis Herman, M.D., *Trauma and Recovery: The Aftermath of Violence - From Domestic Abuse to Political Terror,* Basic Books, 2015

"Knowing trees, I understand the meaning of patience. Knowing grass, I can appreciate persistence."

—Hal Borland, *Countryman: A Summary of Belief,* J.B. Lippincott Company, 1965

1970 ad Infinitum: Some Things Will Always Be the Same—PTSD, Part 24

Loud noises or unexpected noises that are not necessarily loud still scare the hell out of me. I've already discussed the incident in the school cafeteria when a metal chair banged to the floor. A few more incidents follow:

About twenty of Lynda's A Time to Dance students were dancing at a local wine bar. Music was playing, conversation and laughter were loud—a typical noisy bar at ten o'clock in the evening.

I was sitting at a table with friends amidst these decibels.

CLANG, CLANG!

I covered my head and rolled halfway out of my seat toward the floor. Less than five seconds later, I straightened up, exhaled and smiled. A bartender, dumping two or three empty beer bottles into a trash can behind the bar, caused the unexpected and loud noise. Despite the loud environment of usual noises, the unexpected clanging sent me into survival mode for just a few seconds.

I was attending group dance lessons in a hall that Lynda used for such classes. Several helium-filled balloons with attached ribbons from the previous night's party still scraped and bounced across the high ceiling. I sat at a table, changing into my dance shoes.

VRUM VRUM VRUM! VRUM VRUM VRUM! VRUM VRUM VRUM!

I dropped my shoe, covered my head and crouched down onto my haunches next to my chair. A few seconds later, I was raising myself to my seat. I looked at Lynda and her students—they stood with blank stares, wondering what the hell had just happened.

Lynda came over and asked, "Are you okay?"

"Yes, just a little shook, but it'll pass," looking at the balloons above me, realizing they had got caught and released by large, rotating ceiling-fan blades.

"Are you sure?"

"Yeah, really, I should be used to this sort of thing by now, but I never know when I'll react like I just did."

Lynda returned and resumed her lesson.

VRUM VRUM VRUM! VRUM VRUM VRUM! VRUM VRUM VRUM!

This time my response was not as intense, but the noise still startled me. I straightened up and Lynda asked one of her students if he could grab the ribbons and remove the misbehaving balloons. He grabbed a chair, climbed onto the seat and collected the annoying balloons—no more sounds similar to .51 cal machine guns— no more need for flashing into survival mode.

On another day, I was at Lynda's group lessons, assisting her on the second level of a health center. Over the railing and directly below us were dozens of exercise and

261

weight-lifting machines. Many members were present, so the lower floor was quite noisy—a din that became white noise for those of us dancing a few feet above.

I was standing next to Lynda. The ladies were in a line near the railing, and the gentlemen were in a line across from them, against the opposite wall.

CRANG CRANG!

My body spasmed—I grabbed my head and went down on my knees. Three seconds later, realizing where I was—I straightened up. Yes, everyone was looking at me. I said to the class, "Sorry, I never know when that will happen."

"Nothing to be sorry about, Joe," Linda said, "are you okay?"

"Yeah," I said and exhaled, knowing, as everyone else did, that a weight lifter had released his heavy barbell that crashed to the floor.

One or two minutes later, CRANG CRANG!

I reacted in the same way and recovered just as quickly. Lynda walked to the railing and directly below us were weight lifters practicing dead lifts—that they released to crash to the ground. The health center was, by nature, noisy. Lynda was playing music on and off during her lesson. But when the weight lifter dropped those weights, all other noises of the gym's cacophony became insignificant.

During the rest of the lesson, I kept thinking, *okay, it's coming again. Don't be let it surprise you. Don't take cover.* That helped little—I didn't duck for cover, but my entire body spasmed uncontrollably a few more times with each drop.

In between lessons, Lynda spoke to the manager to see if they could do something about the weight lifters' technique. Nothing changed.

So, every Sunday afternoon, I would remind myself—get ready, you'll hear the *cranging*. Sometimes that helped—other times—not so much. My body spasmed uncontrollably—but at least I didn't duck for cover.

I was sitting at the dining room table. Linda was in the kitchen, on the other side of the counter. She dropped a small plastic container onto the countertop's surface and it thumped—my body spasmed. Go figure.

I have realized that this condition will never improve. Unexpected noises, no matter how loud, will continue to cause my exaggerated reactions.

***

A few days before I submitted the manuscript for this memoir, I had another demon dream. In the middle of the night the familiar, dark figures wearing con las returned. This time they were wearing red shirts and dancing in our bedroom's, dresser mirror and TV screen—*in,* not on the mirror or screen.

The images then oozed out of their confines between the edges of mirror and screen and their frames, onto the tops of the dressers—fluid-like puddles in motion, down the sides of the furniture, disappearing onto the floor. I sat up, waiting for them to appear along the sides of the bed. With clenched fists, I waited for them—and they never appeared.

I wasn't as frightened as I usually am; didn't throw the blanket and sheet off of me and jerk up to the kneeling position on the mattress. I didn't disturb Linda. In the morning I asked her if she remembered anything and she did not.

When will these dreams end?

** PTSD **

"While people with PTSD will protect themselves by making sure they are always ready to respond, they can still be easily startled. Health.com writes that they will likely have an exaggerated response when they are surprised or startled, especially if it reminds them of their original trauma.

'Somebody comes up close behind you and you jump a mile,' says Dr. Nitschke to Health.com. 'Before the trauma, you wouldn't have. Hyperarousal can interfere with sleep and concentration, and it may also come out as outbursts of anger.'"

—Katherine George, "The Signs and Symptoms of PTSD," activebeat.com

Live for today—understand the past, forget the mistakes. Remember the lesson. Heal the PTSD and live the life you deserve. Be a SurThriver.

—Tracy Malone, goodreads.com

Memories, a Verse

Misty images and scenes, forms and faces; fleeting names and places, events, circumstances and journeys—all eroded by time's endless scrapings, the foe of recall. But many remain resistant to such forces—appearing as clear as their moment of their making, unfolding or encounter—indelibly etched and preserved.

Their purposes: to verify times, those moments of our existence; to eliminate doubts made clear by asking, "Was that the way it was?" or "Am I forgetting something?"

To satisfy *ponderments*—those what-ifs and maybes, whys and wherefores; to reconsider alternatives, with hesitancy or resolve, that became choices that led to loss or triumph ... either way—the consequences.

To relive—pushing back time-worn curtains, then viewing remnants of our days gone by, whether pleasant or best left unsummoned; then expressed with smiles or tears, fear or curiosity.

To measure and judge our steps in black and white or shades of gray—whether curse or blessing, insanity or balance, terror and turmoil or contentment and tranquility, resulting in sin and

shame or goodness and honor, guilt or innocence,
... grief and pain, or relief and joy.

Elusive delights or torments, shadowy or aglow; these fleeting glimpses of reminiscence—all signs of our evolution and aging ... our mortality. They remain locked in a mysterious dimension to be tapped only for momentary visits or ventures, then depart—gratified or distraught—returning to an uncertain present and the moments that follow, to carry on and for creating many more ... *memories.*

***

Today, I'm in a wonderful position to make many more memories. Retirement is most wonderful. My days go by—writing and dancing keep me busy. I enjoy reading and watching the History Channel and the Cleveland Indians keep me entertained. Also, I never refuse the occasional nap.

But most of all, Linda, my bride, and I have much in common and we spend most of our time together, in love and in life. All is well!

** PTSD **

Instead of saying "I'm damaged, I'm broken, I have trust issues." I say "I'm healing, I'm rediscovering myself, I'm starting over."

—Horacio Jones, declutteryourmind.com

"Everyone forgets that Icarus also flew."

—Jack Gilbert, *Failing and Flying*, Knopf Doubleday
       Publishing Group, 2005

—*Lament for Icarus* by Herbert James Draper, 1898 (public domain).

A Final Eulogy

Yes, Icarus also flew, but many others also flew ... then walked away from millions of landings, except for some that made final landings.

266

I suspect every pilot has realized he or she had gotten away with something big-time, cheated death and scared the hell out of himself—shaking his head in disbelief, apologizing to self or others, then gazing toward heaven and thanking the good Lord and swearing never to commit such sins again.

It would do us well to always remember and never forget such individuals, not only on Veterans Day and Memorial Day, or on individual anniversaries—but every time we see the American flag, every time we hear the Star-Spangled Banner—always remember and never forget those who also flew.

***

Yes, They Also Flew

Yes, Icarus also flew—but too close to the sun—and others flew too close to the enemy. Some challenged Mother Nature or found fault with their abilities or machines, failing ... then falling. In skies of bright blue and white, or storm-gray and dark of night, some were just unlucky.

A few pushed the envelope, clearing the way for others. Some sacrificed themselves for a greater good on missions much larger than themselves. Some instructed and encouraged, passing on lessons to those who followed—then they did the same.

About flight, from nap of the earth to heights absent of gravity, they told their tales. From those bloodied or mangled in wreckage, to those gone in a flash of fire, or traced through DNA remains; from those laid to rest in Arlington to those in thousands of graveyards in Hometown, USA—they all flew.

All along the continuum of flight, famed or forgotten, they remain someone's son or daughter, our nation's patriots, warriors and heroes, from a hundred Main Streets—they all earned wings and exhilarated, took to their seasons in the skies.

We remember them; by worn pictures and home movies, through letters, certificates and medals, with parades and ceremonies; with twenty-one-gun salutes and memorials. We honor those lost lives with fly-overs, by summoning countless memories and letting flow billions of tears …

And they live on—in the hearts of families and friends, in a country's or the world's heart. And we remember … *yes, they also flew.*

***

I shall always remember, and never forget: flight-school classmates, Butch Sears and Jeff Coffin; Cav flyers; Lieutenants Douglas and Dyer, Specialist John Burgess, and Captains Head, and Major Adams.

I shall never forget the thousands of aviators from all the wars—flying in balloons, in wooden and fabric crates, in metal, glass and top-secret alloys, and the astronauts that challenged space in rockets and capsules and black projects we know very little.

Those that disappeared mysteriously—gone without a trace, leaving us with unanswered questions and theories to ponder and speculate … and the unknown or those cloaked in secrecy, awaiting disclosure and the truth.

But most of all … my band of brothers, those Bravo Good Dealers, those Mashers that wore the silver wings of Army Aviation—they shall never be forgotten and always remembered.

So, please remember, as I do, that Icarus once flew … as did millions more.

** Dance **

And when my time comes, consider:

I love to dance and I'd love to be saying goodbye to my friends while the band was playing and they were dancing...I want them to remember I was a dancing man in my day.

—Benjamin Spock

Many believe, including some who are in-the-know, that up to 600 American servicemen were not released by the North Vietnamese after the cease-fire and are still being held captive. However, the Department of Defense has shown that over fifteen hundred personnel remain unaccounted for.

Present Day: Coming Full Circle and Final Ponderments

I still look up whenever I hear the whoppa-whoppa-whoppa of rotor blades beating the air into submission. The bird is rarely a Huey any more—usually some civilian medevac bird I can't identify. But now and then when it is a Huey, I wish I could be with her—yes, wishing just like that eight-year-old kid in 1958.

***

I continue to ask myself questions about Vietnam:

"Why didn't I die at FSB David, on that sniffer mission, or during the rocket attacks, or on countless combat assaults?" And I don't know the answers. How close can you come, so many times … and not die?

"Would I serve in Vietnam again?"

Yes, absolutely, without doubt, without hesitation!

"Would I ever return to Vietnam as a tourist?"

No—the places I'd want to see would be off the beaten path, and others, totally unrecognizable. And I probably couldn't do it in air-conditioned comfort and without back pain and other discomforts. I couldn't take the heat, and my broken-down body would have one serious conversation with my mind about its decision-making process. I'm not nineteen anymore.

"I live my life for each tomorrow

So their memories will live on

Once we were boys, and we were strangers

Now we're brothers and we're men

Someday you'll ask me, was it worth it to be of service in the end?

Well, the blessing, and the curses, yeah, I'd do it all again"

—"Unbroken" written by Jon Bon Jovi, 2019

Present Day: Coming Full Circle and Final Ponderments, Part 2

I guess I've come full circle—on the ground again, looking skywards. Now it's time to say goodbye and thank you for taking the time to learn. I hope I have enlightened you about my war and my ways, and you will understand:

***

Again

I made it home … less than whole—but made it home.

An injured back and PTSD, and memories of things no one should

ever have to see.

And sudden scares by day and demon dreams by night—they'll

always continue to haunt.

Well, they've taken their toll. But I've come to understand, learned and adjusted—and now, fifty-one years later, life is good.

When I'm asked about the war in Vietnam, "If you could choose, would you do it again?"

I don't hesitate to think, don't care about the prices I've paid.

My answer is at the ready, "Of course I would, together with my band of brothers,

Flying mission after mission again, and to the end—our flight school motto remains, 'Above the Best.'"

Then, I add; "Some in the military say, 'God, country, and unit.'"

An admirable mantra, practiced and true, but one I would amend.

I would say, "God, my brothers and I, and country."

Not to diminish, but in battle that's the way it is—it's you and the guy next to you, knowing if you go down—I'm coming for you!

So, to reiterate, "Hell yes, I'd do it again, with my band of Bravo Good Deal brothers—Mashers, one and all."

Give us our Hueys and crews, tell us of your needs, and get the hell out of our way.

We'll do the job—get you in or out, bring you what you need, anytime, anyplace—watch us fly.

And hear us come to you—whoppa whoppa whoppa. That's the sound of my band of brothers and me flying ... *again.*

And for the record, I would like to fly again—just as my buddy Leonardo said. Both of us know:

> *Once you have tasted flight, you will walk the Earth with eyes turned upward, for there you have been, and there you will long to return.*

"The Dance Floor"

"Where age is never a factor and abilities vary,

Where all are admitted and permission is not needed.

Where one direction exists, counterclockwise, and doubt
is to be avoided.

Where inhibitions are prohibited and under the influence
... of music is the rule.

Welcome to ... the dance floor."

—Joseph Michael Sepesy, "The Dance Floor," from
     Word Dances, a Collection of Verses and
     Thoughts about Ballroom Dancing, Lulu Press,
     2014

Final Transmission

Masher 2-4 is QSY. See you at the club ... ahhhh, on the dance floor.

** PTSD **

*One day you will tell your story of how you've overcame what you
are going through now, and it will become part of someone else's
survival guide.*

—Ebraz Ahmed

** Dance **

"Learning the last step shall not come to be—dance is infinite."

—Joseph Michael Sepesy, "Learning the Last Step," from *Word Dances II, Celebration*, 2015

***

May you live in interesting times.

—Ancient Chinese Curse

THE END

Josy

No one who achieves success does so without acknowledging the help of others. The wise and confident acknowledge this help with gratitude.

—Alfred North Whitehead

Acknowledgments

Those Who Made a Difference

Leonardo da Vinci and Igor Sikorsky for their genius, vision, and creativity.

Gary Plotz and Delbert Stewart, who shared the dream of becoming US Army aviators during a time when we knew the inevitable—flying in the war zone of South Vietnam. Rest in peace, Gary. And Delbert—dance on, Star Child!

WORWAC Class 69-49.

Warrant Officers Jeff Coffin, Butch Sears, Bill Schaffer, and Ed Faath.

My Instructor Pilots; Chief Warrant Officers Bobby Cowen, Paul Skyler, and Drew Boudrieau—I guess they saw something in me and had faith in me—otherwise I would have washed out of flight school.

Randy Clark, for being Randy Clark, my best friend, best man, and Masher 2-2, the best helicopter pilot that ever strapped a Huey to his ass.

John Goosman, fellow Bravo Good Dealer, door gunner, and survivor. Thank you for your life's story of duty and service … and success.

My band of brothers, the men of Bravo Company, 227th Assault Helicopter Company, 1st Cavalry Division (AM), for sharing their recollections and stories, and for teaching me how to fly and survive in combat; and those that had the skill, courage and confidence to fly in formation behind me, their Yellow 1.

Major Harold R. Fisher, Masher 6 and Yellow 1, Commanding Officer Bravo Company, 227th Assault Helicopter Battalion, 1st Cavalry Division (AM), August 1970 to January 1971—the best Commanding Officer ever and one fine man. Rest in peace, Mr. Clean.

Chief Warrant Officer Jim Bandy, for his individuality, open-mindedness, and for applying his innate aviator's skills appropriately and with good common sense to befriend me during my third tour of duty in Vietnam.

Warren Motts, Director of the Motts Military Museum in Groveport, Ohio, for his dedication to the United States of America, its history and military traditions, and its veterans and patriots; his wife, Daisy—may she rest in peace; and his daughter, Lori Motts-Byrd, Assistant Director, Motts Military Museum. The artifacts in their museum are as valuable as their human connections—stories brought to life and emotions evoked by Warren and his staff, stories that connect with and touch the visitors.

The Ohio Military Hall of Fame for Valor.

Dr. Thomas Mako, Dr. Mary Ann Echols, Dr. Karpenko—they showed my new band of brothers and me the way. And the members of my severe PTSD therapy group—for their caring, guidance and support, honesty and encouragement.

My dance teacher and dear friend, Lynda Styles, dance instructor and owner of the A Time to Dance studio—she is the reason that dance transformed my life, a beautiful lady with exceptional teaching skills, talent, and passion for ballroom dancing. She cultivated my desire and adapted my broken body to musical movement, making me a dancer.

Terese Hurin, orthotist extraordinaire—without her expertise, determination and friendship I might very well be in a wheelchair.

Green Lantern—he could fly!

Peter Pan—he could fly!

Icarus—he flew!

Daedalus—he enabled Icarus!

Family and Friends

Linda, my beautiful bride, the last puzzle-piece of my life's mural. She insisted I finish this memoir and other projects, understanding that I had to write for endless hours in front of the computer screen, all the while making sure I had snacks and remained hydrated. I must tell her, "I love you so much in my heart!"

Jacqueline Noelle, my daughter—she has succeeded in life. I thank her for the gift of being my daughter. One of those most important gifts occurred on the day we visited Motts Museum when she realized there was much more to her Dad than she had known or appreciated, then expressed her epiphany to Warren Motts. He cried when he told me about that moment with Jackie … and then I cried too.

The entire and extended Sepesy family, for their love, tolerance and understanding, especially during my years of quasi-absence, followed by encouragement and patience to publish this memoir. Thank you, my brothers and sisters, Stevie, Eddie, Kathy, Paul and Monica. I love you so very much!

My dance friends at A Time to Dance; and in Cuyahoga Falls, Ohio, the *Ohio North Coast Jitterbug Connection*, especially the ladies who entrusted themselves to my leading abilities from day one on the dance floor, through my many missteps to today and the thousands of dances that followed with a confident leader.

Lynn Davis, disc jockey at Y-103 in Youngstown, Ohio, for being every veteran's best friend.

The Providers

The dozens of cited authors who enhanced the chapters of this memoir and helped me make more sense of my own PTSD and writing.

Trent Munsey, Masher 3-8, Bravo Good Deal, Aircraft Commander, for providing his story and pictures from his tour of duty in Vietnam. Take care, my friend.

Lieutenant Colonel David W. Eastburn, US Army HQDA OCPA, and the US Army for granting permission to use this memoir's many military images.

The *Youngstown Vindicator* for use of the picture in the first entry, "Years Ago," 8 March 2008—the irony of it all, a surreal hiccup, or an act of fate that was meant to be.

Together We Served, at togetherweserved.com, for providing the photo of Lieutenant Colonel Martha Raye.

"The moment you doubt whether you can fly, you cease forever to be able to do it."

—J. M. Barrie, *Peter Pan*

"In brightest day, in blackest night, no evil shall escape my sight.

Let those who worship evil's might, beware my power ... Green Lantern's light!"

—Alfred Bester, the Green Lantern Corps Oath, from *Green Lantern, Number 9,* 1943

Chronology of Military Service

12 December 1968: Enlistment in US Army.

6 March 1969: Reported for active duty, basic training at Fort Polk, Louisiana.

24 May 1969: Completed basic training and reported for duty at Fort Wolters, Texas.

24 May to 11 September 1969: WOFT (Warrant Officer Flight Training), Primary Phase, Fort Wolters, Texas. Assigned to WORWAC (Warrant Officer Rotary Wing Aviation Course) class 69-49, 10th WOC (Warrant Officer Company). 14 July 1969: Soloed in OH-23 helicopter.

12 September 1969 to 25 February 1970: WOFT, Advanced Phase, Hunter Army Airfield, Fort Stewart, Georgia.

25 February 1970: Received Warrant Officer bars and US Army Aviator wings. (Actual date of warrant and wings is 23 February 1970.)

30 March 1970 to 29 March 1971, First Tour of Duty: Assigned to Bravo Company, 227th Assault Helicopter Battalion, 1st Cavalry Division (Airmobile), Phuoc Vinh, Vietnam.

18 April 1970: Shot down at Fire Support Base Margaret.

1 May through 30 June: Invasion of Cambodia.

14 May 1970: Emergency night resupply at LZ David.

May 1970: One hit through the tail rotor blade, Quan Loi, Vietnam.

14 and 15 June: Incident at Fire Support Base David, Cambodia.

26 June 1970: One .51 caliber hit above tail rotor drive shaft. Released as Aircraft Commander, now Masher 2-4.

27 February 1971: Promoted to Chief Warrant Officer 2.

1 March 1971: Targeted by NVA 37mm anti-aircraft cannon, airburst over Cambodia.

April 1971 to 30 October 1971—Second Tour of Duty: Six-month extension tour with Bravo 227 re-designated as 59th Assault Helicopter Company, 1st Aviation Brigade, Dong Ba Thin and Tuy Hoa, Vietnam.

26 June 1971: Assigned as Yellow 1 for Bravo 227.

5 September 1971: .51 caliber rounds through the cargo deck during combat assault—I should be dead!

24 September 1971: One round through the floor of cargo deck and rotor head.

31 October 1971 to 1 February 1972—Stateside Duty: Assigned to C Troop, 3rd Battalion of the 17th Cavalry Regiment, 82nd Airborne Division, Fort Bragg, North Carolina.

2 February to 1 August 1972: Assigned to the 5th Special Forces Flight Detachment, Fort Bragg, North Carolina.

1 April to 12 June 1972: Instrument Flight Training, Fort Rucker, Alabama.

1 to 14 August 1972: OH-6 transition, Fort Rucker, Alabama.

2 August 1972 to 11 January 1973—Third Tour of Duty: Assigned to the 129th Assault Helicopter Company, 1st Aviation Brigade, Lane Army Airfield, An Son, Vietnam.

12 to 28 January 1973: Assigned to H Troop, 10th Cavalry, 1st Aviation Brigade, Lane Army Airfield, An Son, Vietnam.

29 January to 22 February 1973: Assigned to III Regimental Group Aviation Detachment of the US Embassy, Camp Holloway, Pleiku, Vietnam.

17 February 1973: Separated from active duty with US Army.

29 July 1973 to 2 June 1974: Assigned to N Troop, 107th Armored Cavalry Regiment, Ohio National Guard, Akron, Ohio.

27 June to 17 August 1981: Assigned to Moore Army Airfield, Fort Devens, Massachusetts.

25 December 1985: Honorable discharged from the US Army.

DEPARTMENT OF THE ARMY

THIS IS TO CERTIFY THAT
THE

VALOROUS UNIT AWARD

HAS BEEN AWARDED TO THE

1ST CAVALRY DIVISION (AIRMOBILE) and its assigned and attached units

FOR
EXTRAORDINARY HEROISM IN MILITARY
OPERATIONS AGAINST AN ARMED ENEMY.

IN THE REPUBLIC OF VIETNAM (1 MAY 1970 to 29 JUNE 1970)

GIVEN UNDER MY HAND IN THE CITY OF WASHINGTON
THIS   29TH   DAY OF   JUNE   19 71

Stanley R. Resor
SECRETARY OF THE ARMY

Valorous Unit Award, 1st Cavalry Division (Airmobile), 1 May to
29 June 1970 (Author's private collection).

DEPARTMENT OF THE ARMY
HEADQUARTERS, 7TH SQUADRON, 17TH CAVALRY
APO San Francisco 96226

AVBAУ-C   27 August 1971

SUBJECT: Letter of Appreciation

THRU: Commanding Officer
      268th CAB
      APO SF 96316

TO: CW2 Joseph M. Sepsey
      B/227th
      APO SF 96316

1. I want to express my sincerest appreciation for a job well done for your actions in support of a TAC-E troop insertion on 25 August 1971. Although, originally scheduled to fly a utility mission for CURDS, you were tasked to become the Command and Control aircraft for the insertion.

2. As the mission progressed it became necessary for you to make increasingly more complex decisions involving the usage of aviation assets, aircraft safety, and tactical advice. Throughout the entire mission you maintained a very calm, positive, and professional attitude that provided the example for the rest of the flight. These qualities are uncommon in officers of your grade and experience. I firmly believe that your actions materially affected the outcome of the mission.

3. Once again let me commend your performance. Your actions have reflected favorably upon yourself, your unit, and Army Aviation; keep up the good work.

                                        ERNEST K. SMART
                                        LTC, Armor
                                        Commanding

Letter of Appreciation from Commander, 268th Combat Assault Battalion, 27 August 1971 (Courtesy of the US Army, and author's private collection).

Recommended Reading List

Anton, Frank with Denton, Tommy, *Why Didn't You Get Me Out? The Truth about Heroes, Traitors, & Those Left Behind*, The Summit Publishing Group, Arlington, Texas, 1997.

Appy, Christian G., Patriots: *The Vietnam War Remembered from All Sides*, Penguin Books, New York City, New York, 2003.

Birchim, Barbara, with Clark, Sue, *Is Anybody Listening? A True Story About The POW/MIAs In the Vietnam War*. Author House, Bloomington, Indiana, 2005.

Burkett, B.G., and Whitley, Glenna, *Stolen Valor: How the Vietnam Generation Was Robbed of its Heroes and its History*, Verity Press, 1998.

Coleman, J.D., *Incursion: From America's Chokehold on the NVA Lifelines to the Sacking of the Cambodian Sanctuaries*, St. Martin's Press, New York City, New York, 1991.

Hendon, Bill, *An Enormous Crime: The Definitive Account of American POWs Abandoned in Southeast Asia,* St. Martin's Press, New York City, New York, 2007.

Jenson-Stevenson, Monika, and Stevenson, William, *Kiss the Boys Goodbye: How the United States Betrayed Its Own POWs in Vietnam*, Penguin Books, New York City, New York, 1990.

Moore, Lt. Gen. Harold G. Moore (Ret.), and Galloway, Joseph L. *We Were Soldiers Once ... and Young*, New York City, New York; Random House, 1992.

Moore, Lt. Gen. Harold G. Moore (Ret.), and Galloway, Joseph L. *We Are Soldiers Still*, New York City, New York; HarperCollins Publishers, 2008.

Nolan, Keith William, *Into Cambodia: Spring Campaign, Summer Offensive, 1970*, Presidio Press, Novato, California, 1990.

Sanders, James D., Sauter, Mark A., Kirkwood, R. Cort, *Soldiers of Misfortune: Washington's Secret Betrayal of American POWs in the Soviet Union,* National Press Books, Inc., Bethesda, Maryland, 1992.

Sauter, Mark A., and Sanders, James D., *The Men We Left Behind: Henry Kissinger, the Politics of Deceit and the Tragic Fate of POWs After the Vietnam War*, National Press Books, 1993

Schanberg, Sydney, "McCain and the POW Cover-Up," *The American Conservative*, 1 July 2010.

Shaw, John M, *The Cambodian Campaign: The 1970 Offensive and America's Vietnam War*, University Press of Kansas, 2005.

CPSIA information can be obtained
at www.ICGtesting.com
Printed in the USA
LVHW102144220522
719446LV00018B/266